Demons, Demons, Demons

DEMONS, DEMONS, DEMONS

A CHRISTIAN GUIDE THROUGH THE MURKY MAZE OF THE OCCULT

John P. Newport

 **BROADMAN PRESS**
Nashville, Tennessee

ISBN: 0-8054-5518-3
Library of Congress Catalog Card Number: 78-189503
Dewey Decimal Classification: 133.4
Printed in the United States of America

To

Martha, Frank, and John, Jr.

who

delight and challenge

their parents

FOREWORD

The occult revolution is a fact of modern times. There are many perspectives from which this occult development can be approached, including the descriptive, negative, and sympathetic. This study seeks to include something of the descriptive approach. In addition, it seeks to evaluate the occult, in both a positive and negative way, from the perspective of evangelical Christianity. There are lessons to be learned as well as judgments to be made.

My formal interest in the occult began in relation to teaching assignments at Baylor University some years ago. This interest has continued in relation to courses taught at New Orleans Baptist Seminary and at Southwestern Baptist Theological Seminary.

A former student, Bill Cannon, now an editor of Broadman Press, presented me with a formal proposal to write a book which was to bear the suggested title of *Demons, Demons, Demons.* This proposal and challenge led to more particularized research and study. Students in my classes at Southwestern Baptist Seminary helped in the study by conducting interviews and writing research papers.

An invitation to deliver the Day-Higginbotham Lectures at Southwestern Baptist Seminary in February of 1972 provided further stimulus to formulate concepts and crystallize thinking in regard to the occult. Appreciation is expressed to President Robert Naylor and the faculty of Southwestern Baptist Seminary for the invitation to deliver the lectures and to the members of the Seminary family for their attendance and interest in the lectures.

Material found in this study has been developed in relation to lectures and addresses at several colleges and churches. Especially meaningful has been the interest in a Christian response to the occult by lay people and students in laymen's meetings, student groups, and local churches.

Dr. Keith Wills and the staff of Fleming Library, Southwestern Baptist Seminary, have been especially helpful in the preparation of this volume. Appreciation is in order to Betty Bryant, my secretary, who has been both an efficient typist and a constructive critic. And, as always, I am grateful to my wife Eddie Belle, who has encouraged and helped in so many ways.

JOHN P. NEWPORT
Fort Worth, Texas

CONTENTS

DEMONS, DEMONS, DEMONS

Chapter One

IS THIS
A DEMONIC AGE?

Traditionally demons have been known as fallen angels. A chief angel rebelled and introduced sin into a sinless universe. With him he drew a large number of lower celestial beings (Matt. 25:41; Rev. 12:4). These beings, known as demons, are seen as invisible but real spiritual beings. They roam the universe under their leader, who is known as Satan. Satan is also called Beelzebub, prince of the demons (Matt. 12:24) and the dragon who has his angels (Rev. 12:7). Biblical materials indicate that Satan has his demonic forces well organized like an army (Eph. 6:11,12).[1]

For many people, belief in demons is a part of mankind's nursery furniture. To ask the question, "Is this a demonic age?" would have seemed especially foolish to many "so-called" enlightened Christian theologians and lay people earlier in this century. The eleventh edition of the *Encyclopedia Britannica,* published in 1910, stated as much in its article on the devil. "It may be confidently affirmed that belief in Satan (and obviously his demonic cohorts) is not now generally recognized as an essential article of the Christian faith, nor is it found to be an indispensable element of Christian experience." The article continues by stating that science has explained so many processes of outer nature and of the inner life of man that there is no room left for Satan.[2]

Obviously, Jesus accepted the reality of the demonic. According to the *Britannica* article, however, Jesus either accommodated himself to the primitive views of the time or was limited in his knowledge as a necessary condition of his incarnation.[3] For many early twentieth-century theologians, the demonic concept was a relic of ancient superstitions. It had forever faded out of existence under the strong clear light of reason and common sense.[4]

The calmness of the period following 1910 was interrupted by two world wars. Then came the atomic bomb, Vietnam, political incredibility, the generation gap, the drug culture, and pollution. The radical changes of the 1960's were dramatized, in a theatrical way, when the musical *Hair* burst on America in 1967. Using astrological terms, it affirmed that the old age, the "Age of Pisces," was ending. Charles Reich of Yale, in *The Greening of America*, called the two phases of the older age, "Consciousness I" and "Consciousness II."

The new age now beginning is called by *Hair* the "Age of Aquarius." For Reich, it is "Consciousness III." Aquarius is supposed to be a light, airy sign characterized by aspirations and hope. Since the Bible is closely identified with the Establishment and the Age of Pisces, it is not in general favor. The religious sources are largely Eastern in nature including the Chinese *I*

Ching, Hindu Vedanta scriptures, and Zen Buddhist writings. American Indian lore and astrological books are also popular.

In the early days of the hippie culture and the Aquarian Age, the main emphasis was on Utopian dreams of peace on earth and love. In the early 1960's, the visitor to the Haight-Ashbury area in San Francisco saw thousands of long-haired flower children mixing with gurus, astrologers, Hindu mystics, and soothsayers.[5]

A Time of Radical Change

In recent years, however, a drastic change in outlook has taken place. Anton LaVey, head of a San Francisco group known as the Church of Satan, has been quoted as saying, "The Satanic Age started in 1966. That's when God was proclaimed dead, the Sexual Freedom League came into prominence, and the hippies developed as a free sex culture." [6]

Even though many theologians and lay people have minimized the reality and importance of the concept of personal evil forces, it has always remained a part of evangelical thought. But it receives renewed recognition in times, when, like today, we become aware of the depth and power of evil.

In the 1940's, German theologians such as Karl Heim and Otto Piper were emphasizing the reality of demonic forces. Germany was known as a country of brilliance and achievement in the areas of science, philosophy and culture. These enlightened people had largely rejected the idea of the devil and Antichrist. But Nietzsche and later, Hitler shocked the Germans and all humanity out of their rationalistic slumber into a realization of the depths of demonic power. Accompanying the Nazi take-over in Germany was a flood of occult and magical societies and movements as well as more explicit demonic activities.[7]

An English professor and lay theologian at Oxford University in England, C. S. Lewis, emphasized the work of personal forces of evil in his book entitled *Screwtape Letters,* published in 1942. A famous British philosopher, C. E. M. Joad, had been agnostic about personal supernatural powers and a personal God for thirty years. He had seen evil as being simply the result of economic poverty and lack of education. In his well-known book, *God and Evil,* Joad describes his change in perspective. He came to believe that the power of evil was so intensely real and personal that only a dynamic and personal spiritual power—God—could deliver man from these demonic forces.[8]

A Generation of Diabolical Wickedness

Emil Brunner describes his own pilgrimage and that of many others in similar terms. "It is just because our generation has experienced such diabolical wickedness that many people have abandoned their former 'enlightened' objections to the existence of a 'power of darkness,' and are now prepared to believe in Satan as represented in the Bible." [9] Dale Moody contends that experience in both personal life and cultural life reveal actions that can be attributed neither to God nor to man. The horrors of the Nazi prison camps can hardly be harmonized with the character of honest and pious German people whom one comes to know. And what about race riots among devout and decent people? [10]

Significant achievements of science, such as television and the moving picture screen, can even be used as a tool of demonic arousal and deception. Dr. Arnold Wilson of California, in his interviews with people involved in witchcraft, found that their interest had been aroused by seeing the movie, *Rosemary's Baby.* The novel upon which the movie was based sold over two and one half million copies. Anton LaVey, who played the role of the devil in *Rosemary's Baby,* states that the movie was the best paid commercial for satanism since the Inquisition against witches conducted by the Medieval church. The ending has the heroine accept to her bosom the offspring that was implanted within her by the Devil.[11] The witch-leader, Castavet, cries out in triumph: "God is dead and Satan lives! The year is One, the first year of our Lord, Satan! The year is One, God is done!"[12]

Ritual Murder in California

Is it not ironic that in 1969, ritual murder suggesting black magic was performed against Sharon Tate, the wife of Roman Polanski, director of *Rosemary's Baby,* and four others? The alleged killers, later apprehended, composed a mystical, magical sex cult called the "Manson family." Such a group was suspected since the Polanskis were alleged to have contacts with sex, drug, and witchcraft groups in the Los Angeles area. Sharon, eight-and-one-half months pregnant, was found nude, a breast cut off, and a black magic "X" cut on her stomach. Another victim had been brutally mutilated and had the "X" marks. The Polanskis, and many of their friends, were also deeply involved with Eastern mysticism and spent long evenings reading the hexagrams of *I Ching.* Sharon was a student of black magic, voodoo, astrology, and the occult arts. The neighbors reported that the Polanskis had parties involving altars and white-robed people wearing animal masks.[13]

It is also revealing that a member of the "Manson family," Charles D. "Tex" Watson, was a young man who came from a normal, so-called "Christian," background. A former star athlete, he had come under the dominance of drugs and demonic forces.[14] In all, at least eleven persons died as a result of Manson's demonic activities. Manson had announced (and perhaps believed) that he was—simultaneously—Jesus Christ and Satan. Yet Manson was declared sane. That he was in the power of a "demonic" force cannot easily be denied.[15]

The Manson-Polanski case is obviously an extreme one. But there is evidence that interest in the demonic and the occult is widespread. Astrological themes and echoes of general occultism pervade all phases of the musical *Hair*. Tarot cards, witchcraft, palmistry, numerology, even devil worship are a part of our time. The eager world of fashion and fun has embraced the beads, the flowers, the incense, and the pot of the hippies. Zodiac jewelry, computerized horoscopes, and public exorcisms have become commonplace. Edgar Mitchell had telepathic experiments with Chicago seer Olaf Jonsson during the flight of Apollo 14 and thus has made the occult revolution a cosmic affair.[16] Dennis Wheatley contends that there are 30,000 covens or organized small groups of witches in Great Britain alone. Christian workers in Switzerland report that almost every village has a "witch" or medium who casts spells or brews potions.[17]

Professor Huston Smith of Massachusetts Institute of

Technology tells of the interests of some of the intellectual aristocrats of that scientifically oriented school. Their topics of interest include Asian philosophy, Yoga, Zen, I Ching, brown rice diet, astrology, astral projection, astral bodies, tarot cards, parapsychology, witchcraft, magic, and drugs. This is not an exceptional situation. Andrew Greeley of the University of Chicago reports that in most of the elite universities horoscopes and the prediction of the future by tarot cards are widespread.[18]

The occult has even reached into high places in the organized churches. A Philadelphia spiritualism medium, Arthur Ford, sought to help Bishop James Pike communicate with his dead son. Ford has organized several thousand Protestant clergymen into a Spiritual Frontiers Fellowship. From mainline denominations, these clergymen engage in psychical research and attempts to communicate with the dead through mediums.[19]

Why This New Interest in the Occult?

Various analyses have been made suggesting the reason for this fresh outbreak of interest in the occult. Researchers indicate that many get involved because they are disenchanted with science and technology. Science has helped to make possible frightful developments. Nuclear research has helped to make devastation by nuclear bombs a very real possibility. Better medicine has helped to undergird the population explosion. Runaway technological "progress" may soon exhaust the earth's natural resources. Some ecologists (the catastrophists) give the race twenty-five years under present conditions.[20]

Religion has always been the "sacred canopy" which gives explanations and shelters society from the shock waves of change. The churches have traditionally helped to give people meaning and order in the universe and in history. They have met the needs of people for transcendence, immortality, and liberation. In our time, for many, the traditional churches seem to have lost this power. The churches seem to be too rational, cold, impersonal and remote. This has helped to prepare the way for the occult sciences and the black arts. While church attendance has dropped in major denominations, the occult groups have grown enormously. The occult groups (more than the middle class churches) have furnished a haven for former drug users, disenchanted hippies and yippies, and runaways. The occult has become almost a counter-religion.[21]

One young man recently stated that "the stars and the cards, and even Satan, are more concerned about me than either my draft board, the Pentagon, or the church." [22]

Is This a Counter-Religion?

In itself, states Brunner, the sphere of occult magic may be neutral. Interest in the subject, if it is of a purely scientific or historical nature, certainly has nothing directly to do with the demonic. The main interest in the occult in our time, however, is as a counter-religion. When the magical is dabbled with in this way, it opens the way, suggests Wheatley, to the influence of the powers of darkness—to the demonic. The devil works through the luminous halo, through that which fascinates and allures. He prefers to fly high rather than low! [23]

The well-known theologian, Paul Tillich, affirms that we are in a demonic age. Tillich understands the demonic, however, in impersonal and metaphysical terms rather than in personal terms. For Tillich, God, who is essentially form-creating, has also a form-destroying aspect in the inexhaustible depths of being. Historical man, with this divine stuff in his being, uses his creative powers for his own destruction. This view tends to place the actual responsibility for sin and evil much more upon God than upon created fallen beings and man.[24]

There are many other prominent theologians and biblical scholars, however, such as Helmut Thielicke, Otto Piper, Emil Brunner, James Kallas, and Eric Rust who disagree with Tillich. For them, the view that a personal Satan and his fallen angels tempt and frustrate men makes sense in today's world. This view is more in keeping with biblical teaching, human experience, and a consistent philosophy. For example, this biblical view avoids the dangers of both monism and dualism. It helps to account for temptation and evil, but preserves man's personal responsibility.[25]

Helmut Thielicke, the prominent German theologian, is especially emphatic in his affirmation that the present age is influenced negatively by personal demonic forces. In the demonic activities of the Nazis and in more recent activities, he sees a correspondence to the historical situation which is portrayed in the book of Revelation. In fact, Thielicke contends that anyone who would understand history and our age must be in possession of the category of the demonic. Although the Bible does not claim to "explain" evil, it does "describe" it as personal. For Thielicke, the personal view

is true to his own experience—he encounters evil as
personal demonic power. He notes, however, that it is
only in the light of God's revelation in Christ that the
demonic can be understood.[26]

Should You Believe in Personal Demonic Powers?

Theologians, such as Thielicke, do not accept the explanation of the demonic which was suggested by the
Encyclopedia Britannica and which is popular among
some writers today. This view teaches that the conception of the satanic and the demonic is only a part of a
rather primitive, first century world-picture. Men no
longer accept the idea of a flat earth and a three-storied
universe—why should they accept the idea of personal
demonic powers? For Thielicke, Rust, and others, however, the concept of the demonic and a personal Satan
is an essential part of a perennially valid biblical world-
view. This world-view includes the doctrines of creation, God-man relations (sin and salvation), and
consummation. The demonic is related in an especially
close way to the themes of sin and judgment.[27] Although scientific world-pictures change often, the biblical world-view continues to explain God-man and
man-man relationships. Through the thought forms of
the first century, we are given a description of personal
demonic forces, organized around a personal Satan,
operating in history—both on a collective and personal
level. This view is still valid today.[28]

For Eric Rust, the well-known British theologian, it
is necessary to ascribe personal will to the parasitic
presence of evil in the divine creation. Furthermore,
this view is nearer to the biblical truth and human
experience than attempts, such as the one made by

Tillich, to give a metaphysical explanation of evil in terms of some cosmic principle within the totality of being. There is evidence of a personal evil force which exerts purposive activity in an organized way.[29]

Emil Brunner agrees with Rust. The Bible plainly states that there is a personal force of a superhuman kind who stands over against man. He is an "objective reality" who is objectively encountered. He is not merely a reality within the mind. Satan is a spiritual force who works directly on the spirit. He does not have to have mediations. His method of influence is occult or secretive. He is both one and many. He wills to remain hidden. He pretends to be an "angel of light." [30]

Evidence has already been cited for the close relationship between interest in the occult (spiritualism, clairvoyance, divination, foretelling, magic, reincarnation, astrology) and the satanic and demonic. Brunner reports, on the testimony of numerous people, that the area of the occult has been an opening for satanic attacks. For many, the occult seems to be illuminated by a magical radiance. It assumes an incomprehensible force of attraction. This seems to be a part of the strategy of Satan. The spellbinding effects of the occult are so strong that they defeat all the efforts of the spiritual adviser until he dares to make a frontal attack.[31]

Listening to Seducing Spirits

Other scholars, however, believe that much of the interest in the occult issues directly from Satan for man's harm. It is pointed out that the Apostle Paul in 1 Timothy 4:1,2 teaches that in the latter times some will depart from the faith by listening to or devoting themselves to "seducing spirits." In addition, reference is made to the "doctrines of demons." An example of one of the "doctrines of demons" in Paul's day was an incipient gnosticism which involved an ascetic legalism (1 Tim. 4:3–6). According to this approach, the apostle could have just as appropriately used one of the occultic practices of today as an example of "doctrines of demons." First John 4:1–3 warns Christians to prove (test) the spirits to see if they are of God. The basic criterion for testing is a person's relation to and understanding of Jesus Christ as the God-man.[32] G. Campbell Morgan, among others, suggests that demonic activity is responsible for the upsurge of much of the occult in our time.[33]

In one sense, from the biblical perspective, every age is demonic. Each age, until the second coming of Christ, is the scene of the cosmic struggle between the kingdom of God and the personal forces of evil. Satan and demonic powers are active in every period of history and use human beings and nations as their instruments.

Jesus Warns the Demonic Evil Will Increase

However, Jesus and the chief New Testament writers appear to indicate that the demonic evil which is powerful in every age will become more intense as we approach the last days of history.[34] Are the occult developments of our time indications of this intensification of demonic activity? In Mark 13 and Matthew 24, Jesus indicated that the kingdom of God would not be established at once, but that the future would involve a period of wars, conflicts, earthquakes, and persecutions, even to the point of death. Many people, said Jesus, will come in my name and seek to lead you astray (Mark

13:5b,6). One method to be used to create confusion is the showing of signs and wonders (Mark 13:22). Early incarnations of evil foreshadow a last supreme concentration of the devil. The Antichrist will afflict the people of God. After this will occur the coming of Christ and the gathering of the saints into the kingdom of God.[35]

The apostle Paul in 2 Thessalonians 2:1–12 also suggests that one stage in the apocalyptic drama is apostasy or a falling away (2:3). Another is the appearance of the man of lawlessness with pretended powers and wonders. Just as Christ has his first and second comings, so the lawless one has his coming. His coming is to be an expression of the activity of Satan (2:8,9). Here miracles are not the signs of the working of God, but expressions of the power of evil spirits (2:9).

As has already been indicated, the apostle Paul states that in the last days men will give heed to seducing spirits and doctrines of devils (1 Tim. 4:1). Is Paul predicting the situation which we find today in regard to the occult?[36] Is it possible that the rising evidence of demonism in various forms has an eschatological import? Is it because the second coming of Christ is near, that we are witnessing stepped up satanic activity? Is this a clue to the present worldwide unrest in every area of life?

At least we can be sure that we are true to the spirit of Paul in this passage when we think of the conflict between Christ and the powers of evil as growing in intensity as history develops. We are also true to the spirit of Paul when we think of the forces of evil as deifying themselves and presenting themselves as ways of salvation for mankind.

The Last-Ditch Stand of the Demonic?

Thielicke suggests that when Christ walked the earth
the demonic powers gathered themselves together in
one last effort to preserve their doomed kingdom. The
nearer the return of Christ, the more energetically Satan mobilizes his last reserves, until the demonic ex-
cesses reach their climax and Christ returns.[37] Martin
Luther once said that the devil obviously feels the day
of the end. That is why he thinks he had better disturb
the dregs.[38]

Arthur Smethurst suggests that satanic activity is a
possible answer to certain biological frustrations which
baffle scientists.[39] G. B. Caird agrees, and contends that
Satan operates in the world of nature, at subhuman
levels. Paul hints at this in Romans 8:20–22 when he
talks of the whole creation being held in the bondage
of corruption.[40]

The same basic structure of thought concerning last
things, which appeared in Mark 13, Matthew 24, and
2 Thessalonians 2, appears also in the book of Revelation. There will be a time of preliminary troubles in
human society and in nature (the seven seals, Rev. 5–8).
This will be followed by a short but terrible time of
great tribulation (the seven trumpets and bowls, and
the beast, Rev. 8–16). In the preliminary evil period,
however, there will still be a dynamic preaching of the
gospel (Mark 13:10, Matt. 24:14). The course of history
is not to be one of unrelieved evil when God's people
are surrendered helplessly into the hands of hostile
powers.

A number of scholars contend that the white horse
of Revelation 6:2 symbolizes the fact that there will be

a dynamic gospel mission in all of the world until the end alongside the development of evil. John does not look for the full coming of God's final kingdom and the complete righting of the world's evils short of the return of Christ. However, as bearers of the gospel, he expected the Christians to see victories won by the power of the gospel.

If the Revelation of John is to have dynamic meaning for today, which is assumed, it is to be seen as more than a description of the hopes which the early Christians of Asia had in regard to deliverance from Rome. Is it not both historical and future-oriented? I would follow G. Beasley-Murray in contending that it is. The beast is both Rome and the final Antichrist—and any intervening demonic power which the church must face. There was tribulation in the first century. There will be a final tribulation, but the concept of tribulation also includes all of the continuing tribulations of history. The book of Revelation speaks not only of the first century events but of the last great events of history. It does not give a time chart, but it does tell of dynamic trends and movements. The demonic power of Rome which persecuted the early Christians is but a preliminary incarnation of the final evil powers.[42]

It is obvious that the biblical writers teach that history will be tension filled—between an evil and hostile environment and a dynamic gospel proclamation and practice. As Thielicke indicates, without an understanding of the demonic activity, there is no full understanding of the dynamics of history. In the book of Revelation, chapter 12, John describes the great warfare in the spiritual world. The difficulties of the church on earth are a manifestation in history of a spiritual battle. Behind the beast is the dragon—the devil, Satan—whose aim is to frustrate the rule of God through his Messiah.[43]

A Parody of Christ

In Revelation 13, John describes the persecution of the church by the Antichrist who has been foreshadowed in certain Roman rulers and other totalitarian dictators. In Revelation 13:11, the second beast makes a parody of Christ—he appears as a lamb, but he speaks as a dragon. Even religion may be demonic. Many people call the occult a religion or a counter-religion. In Revelation 13:13-14a, the beast (later to be called the false prophet) employs pseudo-miracles and magic.[44]

Is this a demonic age? It is in the sense that there appears to be a struggle—both cosmic and historical—moving toward a crescendo—between the forces of God and the forces of the satanic powers.

This development can be seen in a dramatic way in the contemporary youth culture. There is a struggle between those young people using folk-rock music who look to Jesus for inspiration and those who look to Satan for meaning. There are two opposing forces even among the most "strung-out" of our young people. The lyrics of certain rock groups never stop telling about Jesus and his love. The lyrics of such groups as the Rolling Stones talk about sympathy for the devil. The *Black Sabbath,* a rock celebration of sorcery and witchcraft, has had international appeal. The Jesus Movement is all out for Christ, and other groups are all out for the devil. These developments remind us of what we have just seen in the book of Revelation.

The Apocalyptic Young

Brunner contends that the more dynamic the proclamation of the gospel, the more violent is the hostility
of Satan.[46] The "Jesus Freaks" are aggressive, and demonic forces are hostile. Some of the new Jesus Movement sects, however, are not only aggressive in
preaching the gospel, but they are also anti-cultural.
They tend to withdraw, like the ancient Egyptian
monks, to await the End. Apocalyptic eschatology is a
part of their speech and permeates their music and
writing. The movement called "The Children of God,"
for example, is anticipating the almost immediate coming of Jesus Christ. For them, the war, the rape of the
environment, government lies, and the apathetic
churches are causes for withdrawal and evidences of
the impending end.[47]

It would be well for the Jesus Movement as well as
those interested in the apocalyptic teachings in the
more traditional churches, to remember that Jesus was
never interested in the future for its own sake. He
speaks of the future because of its import upon the
present. Even the discourse on Last Things in Matthew
25 had an ethical objective: to exhort to watchfulness
and readiness for the end.[48] In light of the impending
end, the book of Revelation exhorts the people in the
churches to repent.

Another definite emphasis of Jesus, as well as Paul
and John, is that there is to be no time-setting for apocalyptic events. In the words of Barnhouse, all we can
look for in contemporary events are tendencies which
point in the direction of the prophetic scriptures.[49]

This means, also, that there is to be no escapism and

despair. Although the dominion which Satan holds over this earth precludes any kind of easy optimism, neither is there reason for dark pessimism. Satan can never increase his might beyond the measure granted to him by God. God by his "common grace" comes again and again into history to strengthen the powers of goodness. The "fulness of time," when Jesus came into history, was not when man had reached perfection, but rather the time when divine help was supremely needed. Perhaps God will grant spiritual outbreaks in history before the Second Coming.[50] In any case, it is our duty and opportunity to devise frameworks of justice and to do deeds of love in the name and power of Christ in the interim which is given to us. We need to provide exciting new versions of Christian life styles. Above all, we must become involved in a dynamic, evangelistic, and missionary proclamation of the glories of Christ.

You Are Still Responsible, Christian

And we must also remember that belief in a personal Satan and the reality of demonic forces do not destroy human responsibility. Satan can tempt, but he cannot force. He is a created being—not co-equal with God. He is not to be our scapegoat to remove our blame. Extreme credulity is as undesirable as extreme reductionism. We are not to transfer the source of evil to Satan only.

It will be our purpose in the following chapters to seek to describe and evaluate representative, contemporary movements in the area of the occult in the light of basic biblical guidelines. And guidance is needed! Not all elements of the occult developments are bad in themselves. In a materialistic culture, they have revived interest in the spiritual world. These occult developments also reveal a groping and hunger for meaningful standards to guide life and give meaning to activities. Cold and formal churches can learn lessons from these developments.[51]

As has been indicated, however, demonic forces are abroad and the doctrines of the occult movements must be tested and a new and a more dynamic Christian response indicated.

Chapter Two

WHAT ABOUT MAGIC AND WITCHCRAFT?

Any comprehensive consideration of the occult in today's world would have to include magic and witchcraft. For many, such a study is real fun. For some, it almost assumes the form of polite pornography. Magic —especially black magic—and witchcraft are much more serious, however, than the latest fad to titillate and shock. Witchcraft has been largely underground in this country since the Salem witch trials in the seventeenth century. Now it has come up again. And it is more than fun and games! It has profound and important religious and theological implications.

Many conservative authors would not think it helpful to see anything in witchcraft and magic except that which is satanic and demonic. I believe it will be helpful, however, to see witchcraft and magic in historical perspective and from the viewpoint of representative approaches before we come to our final biblical and theological evaluation in Chapter three.

Magic—black and white—and witchcraft are dynamically alive in most of the world today. The Manson murders, already mentioned, were related to black magic. The success of the film *Rosemary's Baby* reveals how much Americans like this sort of thing. Witchcraft has also appeared on television *(Bewitched)*, and in comic strips *(Broomhilda)*, as well as in magazines, newspapers, and other media.

Black Magic's "Second Coming"

Arthur Lyons calls this present-day development the "second coming" of black magic and witchcraft. The hippie culture and college campuses are centers of this movement. The students sport beads and amulets that supposedly have magical powers. Many firmly believe in witchcraft.[1]

Courses in witchcraft are being offered in as many as sixty-eight institutions of higher learning. At New York University so many students signed up for "Witchcraft, Magic, and Sorcery" that classes had to be moved to one of the school's largest lecture halls.[2] Who has not seen interviews on radio and television with self-claimed witches? Even the daily newspapers offer tips on how to cast curses or spells![3]

Kurt Koch, well-known German specialist in the occult, reports hundreds of counselees who have been oppressed or harassed through black magical powers. Others report that they have been helped through white magic. Missionaries report evidences of the supernatural power of witchcraft in foreign lands. I found this especially prevalent in Korea.

Beaten to Death as a Witch

Both England and Europe report dynamic witch movements. Bernadette Hasler, a seventeen-year-old

Swiss girl, was beaten to death in 1966 because she was charged with sexual intercourse with Satan. This weird case came to light at the Zurich trial of a defrocked German priest and five of his followers. They were charged with murdering Miss Hasler while trying to exorcise or drive out a demon from her.[4]

Christian workers in Switzerland have reported that there is scarcely a village in that beautiful country that does not have a "witch" or medium. They cast spells and brew potions. Nearly every village in Italy has a specialist in the occult.[5] Obviously magic and witchcraft do not constitute an isolated phenomenon. They manifest something terrifying, something demonic!

In all fairness, it should be noted that some reputable scholars and witchcraft specialists contend that many modern followers of magic and witchcraft caricature historic magic and witchcraft.[6] Following the leadership of Margaret Murray, a British anthropologist, these scholars state that witchcraft was an organized religion or craft in Europe before Christianity. These scholars admit that the black witches were involved in weird and questionable practices in the medieval period. They claim, however, that the white witches practiced a more constructive fertility or nature religion.[7]

Was Witch Persecution Unfair?

According to witchcraft specialist Gerald Gardner, medieval Christians instituted severe persecution of all kinds of witches. The Christian missionaries ascribed the witchcraft which they found among the pagans to the work of the devil. Kerr suggests that questions asked the persecuted witches brought forth wanted affirmative answers as the hot iron passed in front of their eyes. Perhaps some of the witchcraft practices were not as bad as the forced answers described. Did the persecutors put the words in the mouth of the people? As the mass hysteria developed, more evil was admitted, and thus more persecution seemed justified.[8]

Too Much Sympathy for Witches?

It is the opinion of another scholar, Arthur Lyons, however, that many researchers such as Hans Holzer and Gerald Gardner, are too sympathetic with witchcraft. They have done a "whitewash job" on the entire field. According to Lyons, extensive black magic groups have existed historically. They exist today and continue to practice black magic on a large scale.[9]

Unfortunately, so much contradictory and superficial material about witchcraft is published that it is difficult to describe in a completely satisfactory way either ancient or modern witchcraft. It is not questioned, however, that thousands of people around the world profess to be witches and practice magic.[10]

What Are We Talking About?

It will be helpful, before going further, to define terms. Magic is foundational in the occult arts. A key idea of magical beliefs, of which witchcraft is a form, is that unseen Powers exist. By performing the right kind of ritual, these Powers can be contacted and forced to assist.[11] Magic, therefore, is the attempt by a practitioner to manipulate universal forces. Conservative Christian authors would define magic as the divinely forbidden art of bringing about results beyond human power by recourse to superhuman spirit agencies (Satan and demons). For the conservative, magic is deception and superstition even if it does not enlist the power of darkness. It possesses the character of diabolic miracle when it does. Parapsychologists would have a different explanation.

Many Superstitions Derive from Magic

Magic is as old as man. Most superstitions are ritualized patterns of magical behavior, the reasons for which have become obscure by centuries of custom. Why, for example, does carrying a rabbit's foot bring luck? [12]

Obviously, the magical approach is different from the biblical perspective. In the biblical religion, properly understood, Almighty God is praised, reverenced, acknowledged as power, and supplicated. In supplication, a person does not seek to force God's will. As the sovereign God, he can use his own free will in regard to answering a human request.[13] Professing Christians sometimes resort to semi-magical practices when they talk about "How to get success through religion" or "How to get rich through prayer" or "How to get where I want to go through religion."

There Are Two Kinds: Black and White

Basically, magic and witchcraft are divided into white and black. White witches are supposed to use their magic to help others and to do good. Black witches try to hurt and harm others. Black magic involves the direct solicitation and help of demons, specifically the devil. It is the most terrible and powerful form of occult art. It majors in enchantment for persecution and vengeance. It also seeks to employ diabolical powers for defense and healing. It is widely practiced in Tibet.

Sympathetic, Contact, and Contagion Magic

Magic is performed sympathetically through a personal belonging or effigy, through incantations (chants and rituals) and through the magic of talismans (jewelry, bones, etc.). Sympathetic magic works through the principle of analogy. For example, it performs a ceremony that imitates the desired end. A Voodoo practitioner puts pins in a doll to cause death or pain to his intended victim.

Contact magic is based on the belief that things that have been in contact remain in a kind of direct association, even though physically separated. Thus, for example, by injuring a piece of clothing, one seeks to induce injury to the person who has at some time worn that clothing. Contagion magic also uses a piece of a person's clothing to secure that person's vital force.[14]

Sympathetic and contagion magic are closely related to the sacramental rituals which are observed in all the world religions. These sacramental practices can easily cross the border back into magical superstition. Examples include crossing oneself in times of danger, wearing medals for protection, or burning blessing candles.[15]

White Magic in the Middle Ages

White magic was widely practiced during the Middle Ages using Christian symbols and crosses. It also used incantations of the Trinity and the Lord's Prayer. The

Mass was believed by the Christians to be the ultimate magical ritual. Long pilgrimages were made to shrines where holy objects were kept.[16] Conservative authors contend that white magic is black magic in pious masquerade. It uses, in a magical way, the name of God, Christ, and the Holy Spirit and Bible phrases, but is demonic in character. These scholars remember the Apostle Paul's statement in Second Corinthians 11:14 that Satan often comes as an angel of light.

The early yippies, who wanted to rebel against the structures of the church and society, found a convenient framework in black magic. Many see the revolt emphasis as important in the revival of black magic interest today. A Black Mass is a degradation of the "God of the Establishment Religion." [17]

Black magic has apparently existed in all cultures. The concept of Satan, however, is primarily related to the Hebrew-Christian tradition and is not universal—at least as a fully developed doctrine. From the perspective of those who say that they follow the ancient religion of witchcraft, not all black magicians are Satanists. From a conservative Christian perspective, most black magic is seen as Satan inspired.[18]

Wherever the early Christian missionaries went in the early centuries, they found the peasants engaged in what is called "Old Religion" and worshipping the horned gods of fertility. These fertility gods became the symbols of resistance to Christianity. The people following them did not convert easily. It is easy to see why the fertility gods were soon condemned as representatives of anti-Christ or Satan.[19] Consequently, the pre-Christian ceremonies, which were originally known as witchcraft, came to be termed devil worship.[20]

"Baptizing" Pagan Practices Did Not Work

At first, the medieval church tried to "baptize" and adapt pagan ceremonies. An example of this is the adaptation of the pagan fertility goddesses into the Mary cult of the medieval church. As it became stronger, however, the church decided to take a more aggressive negative approach toward paganism. In 1215, Pope Innocent III created the Inquisition to ferret out witches along with heretics. The first woman was burned alive in 1275, having been accused of witchcraft and sexual relations with the devil.[21]

The Motivations of the Peasants

Unfortunately, many of the feudal lords who were identified with the church were unjust and cruel. The celibacy craze in the medieval monasteries tended to identify the clergy with asceticism, a joyless approach to life, and a negatión of the lively arts. The Christian God, for the peasants, thus became identified with the oppression of the feudal lords and the asceticism of the medieval monks.[22] A similar development has taken place in our time. Christianity has become identified with the status quo, joyless living, and negativism. To seek to correct this image some contemporary authors may have gone to an almost opposite extreme. Such authors and their writings include Sam Keen's, *To A Dancing God,* Harvey Cox's *Feast of Fools* and John Killinger's *Leave it to the Spirit.*

The "Old Religion" and the "Horned God"

The peasants longed for a return to the "Old Religion" and its horned god of fertility. The church had changed their old horned god's name to the devil. Thus, thousands of peasants were designated as devil worshippers. This is one explanation of the rise of the medieval phenomenon known as devil worship.[23] A somewhat similar development was to take place later in Russia. The church became identified with the oppressive Czars and thus lost most of the common people to Lenin and the Communist cause.

European witches—and American witches who are related to the same roots—developed fascinating organizational forms and ritual ceremonies. The evidence, like the material available concerning the dissenting religious groups in the Middle Ages, is colored by the viewpoint of the persecuting church which furnishes most of the records.[24] From the witchcraft confessions and the handbooks of witchcraft trials, a general impression of witches and their activities emerges. At least we have descriptions of the popular beliefs about witches.[25]

Details About Witchcraft

A coven is usually considered to be the standard unit of witchcraft. Some scholars insist that the coven is a late development. At least it is a unit used today. It consists of twelve witches (six male, six female) and a high priest or priestess. Is this a parody of Christ and the twelve apostles? Some say that it is. The male leader sometimes impersonates the devil. He oftentimes dresses as a black ram.

The meeting which is primarily concerned with business is called "the Esbat." The more religious meeting is "the Sabbat." The religious meetings are held each month—usually when the moon is full. The really big meeting is held on Halloween (October 31).[26] The extensive research of Arthur Lyons reveals many interesting facts concerning these services. Prior to the religious service, roll calls are conducted. New members have to make an open disavowal of the Christian faith and enter into a pact with the devil. The witches' mark, a permanent scar or tattoo, is then placed under the member's arm or on the genitals. During the Middle Ages, searching for these marks on the bodies of the accused became sadistic. It gave the self-righteous interrogators great opportunity to peer at human nakedness.[27]

Historically, meetings were held in secret places or even in churchyards. They began at midnight, ending with the first flush of the dawn's light.[28]

The religious service followed a "liturgy of evil." A black animal was sacrificed. Homage was paid to the leader representing Satan by placing a ritual kiss on his buttocks. After they conducted a ritualized parody of the Catholic Mass, they had a feast. Then came a wild orgy of dancing—often obscene. Theoretically, Satan was to copulate with every woman present. An artificial leather phallus was probably used for at least part of this ritual.[29]

Perverted Sexual Practices

After the devil had had his due, the men and women fell on each other in a mad debauchery, indulging in every possible heterosexual perversion. In exceptional cases, child-sacrifices and cannibalism were included.[30]

Witches are taught and believe that a person's body contains a power reservoir. Clothes hamper this "power field," and, therefore, the witch must work naked. The power is best released by dancing around in a circle, singing and shouting.[31] Historically, witches anointed themselves with a salve containing what we now call psychedelic drugs. This gave them the feeling of flying through the air. This was the original "high." [32] Today people talk of getting "high" at cocktail and drug parties.

By the end of the seventeenth century, the Reformation and the scientific renaissance brought an end to the cruelest part of the inquisition approach to witchcraft. According to Martin Ebon, witches were lynched in Mexico as late as 1968. France burned its last witch in 1745. It was 1775 before Germany beheaded her last witch.[33]

The Black Mass

The main practices of the witch movement moved indoors in the form of the Black Mass. The Catholic service was changed to substitute "Satan" for "God" and "evil" for "good." The altar was either a naked woman or a coffin. The consecrated wine was replaced by urine and semen. The bread was replaced by dried feces. These are bodily products, as opposed to spiritual, and as such are pleasing to Satan, who is a carnal deity.[34] A semiauthentic recreation of a Black Mass can be heard on the album *Witchcraft*. It is recorded by a "put-on" group in Chicago called "The Coven." [35]

The Black Mass is clearly a case of ritual rebellion against the established church. The services were oftentimes enlarged to include rebaptism in the devil's name and a reading of the Lord's Prayer backward.[36]

Similar services are widespread today in the meetings of the Church of Satan and similar witchcraft and satanist groups.

For the peasant, who saw himself victimized by a cold, monolithic church, the Black Mass was a means of striking back. It was a way of venting hatred.[37]

The upper classes devised even more horrible Black Masses and services in the fifteenth, sixteenth, seventeenth and even into the eighteenth centuries. These services constituted a prototype for the writings of Marquis de Sade, whose fictional works such as *Justine* have gained wide attention in our time. In the novel *Justine* de Sade includes a lengthy passage describing a Gallic Black Mass.

The Depths of Satanic Depravity

In France, Gilles de Laval, the escort of Joan of Arc and the original Bluebeard, celebrated notorious Black Masses. He sacrificed young boys to Satan after he brutally used them in a homosexual fashion. In the service he used copper vessels filled with the blood of his victims. Laval was burned alive in 1440 for the murder of two hundred children. He needed their blood for the satanic masses, he said. Louis XIV's mistress, Madame de Montespan, two centuries later, had Black Masses conducted in which children's throats were cut to furnish blood for the chalice. These masses were love masses where she acted as a naked altar. She believed that through the magic of these masses she could "win and maintain" the favor of the king.[38]

In the eighteenth century, in Great Britain, Black Masses were conducted by the well-known Hellfire Clubs. The masses were conducted over an altar consisting of a naked girl. The monks of these groups, known as the "Unholy Twelve," were influential political and literary figures, including a Prime Minister of England.[39]

Witchcraft in the United States

The story of witchcraft in the United States is well-known. It existed from the beginning of the Puritan settlements. Persecutions against witchcraft were made in most of the states. The Puritans found New England a land of cold winters and inhospitable terrain. They were surrounded by the Indians. For many, this situation was seen as the devil plaguing them. Why was God's wrath upon them? Cotton Mather and others taught that Judgment Day was at hand, and Satan was stepping up his activities in one last desperate move.[40]

This was something of the background for the 1692 witch trials in Salem, Massachusetts. A West Indian maidservant told of her intercourse with demonic forces. The hysteria spread. Most scholars suggest that the Satanism of Salem is not the Satanism of the historic "Old Religion" of Europe. In the United States, the nearest thing to the original witchcraft of Europe is probably the witchcraft of the Ozarks. It came from the oral tradition which had been brought over from England.

Arthur Miller, the American dramatist, in his play, the *Crucible*, propounds the "Scapegoat theory" as an explanation of Salem. Psychologists see sexually disturbed girls and sexually frustrated clergymen as a partial explanation.[42] Others see the Salem incident as mass hysteria. But underneath the sociological and psychological causes, could there not run a stream of darkness, a delusion of Satan? It all began in Salem with a tampering with the occult.[43]

A Mass Underground Movement

The Salem witchcraft trials were in 1692. What of today? Earlier it was suggested, in the words of Arthur Lyons, that the demonic has had a "second coming" in our time. During the past decade, witch cults have sprung up with such rapidity that devil worship seems to be taking on the aspects of a mass underground movement.

Because of the secrecy of the groups, the number of the involved is hard to estimate.[44] At least 5,000 witches are said to practice in New York and 10,000 in Los Angeles. Richard Woods suggests that in the United States there are perhaps as many as one hundred thousand witches in all which is about one-half the number of clergymen or physicians.[45] The Witches' Cauldron, founded early in 1970, is doing a booming business in incense, witch bracelets, talismans, and other "metaphysical supplies." Scattered stores now sell sorcerer's staples such as the lathane knife for spells, magic oils, black cat bone, the heart of swallow, and black henbane. Once a few were interested, now almost everybody is concerned, says Zolar, a long-time occult supplier. The Fort Worth, Texas, public library system has published a brochure describing the many books available in their libraries on witchcraft.[46]

The Expanding Witchcraft Movement

Interstate and international witchcraft groups are expanding rapidly. Witchcraft is out in the open in England, since the ancient British Witchcraft Act was repealed in 1951. Schools of witchcraft are popular in England. The R.O.W.W. (Royal Order of Warlocks and Witches), with headquarters in Miami, Florida, claims a worldwide, secret membership.[47] In France, thousands of people spend two hundred million dollars a year consulting 60,000 sorcerers. Some 10,000 witch doctors are malpracticing in Germany for high fees. Dozens of lawsuits concerning malpractice are before the German courts each year.[48] In Puerto Rico, witchcraft is involved in labor union elections. Witchcraft is almost overwhelming in its power in modern Brazil.[49]

As we have already noted, from a historical or sociological perspective, the witchcraft of the medieval European peasants was a messianic movement spurred on by a repressive social system which was identified with the church. The peasants turned to the only image of rebellion that they knew—Satan. For the European aristocrat, Black Masses relieved boredom, allowed him to ritualize his perversions, and hopefully helped him to get either vengeance or position.[50]

The "New" Witchcraft

The new witchcraft is somewhat different. The hippie drug culture in the United States has done much to influence and popularize some new emphases in witchcraft. Since the churches in the United States are not as identified with the coercive power structures as was the medieval church, Black Masses in some cases take the form of anti-war demonstrations and "love-ins." If some type of religious orthodoxy is dominant in a particular geographical area, such as Salt Lake City, Black Masses tend to be more anti-Christian.[51]

Sex, now more permissive among youth, is probably not as important in witchcraft as it was in the Middle Ages. Leaders still use the witchcraft movement, however, as a vehicle to get and exert power.[52] Reincarnation is bigger than ever before in witchcraft because of Eastern influences.

Romanticizing the Devil

The devil, in today's witchcraft, tends to be romanticized. He is seen by many as more powerful and immediate than God. In reaction to the competitive materialism of American society, witchcraft tends to be more mystical than in the past.[53]

The new witchcraft is also seeking to create a more positive image. Sybil Leek, a prominent British witch who spends much of her time in the United States, suggests that witchcraft is a fulfilling religion requiring a mature decision.[54] Hans Holzer seeks to maintain that the white witches do not use their powers for personal gain. This brand of witchcraft, according to Holzer, employs "white" magic to "raise the natural powers" latent in the human body and spirit. In fact, many contemporary witches claim that their divinities are not personal beings, but represent abstract principles of life, love, fertility and nature. The witches, however, do try to "summon the power" to help members find a mate, secure a job, pass an exam, or gain physical healing. These modern white witches claim that their meetings do not end in an unbridled orgy, but with coffee and cake.[55] Mrs. Leek teaches that, in witchcraft, a person can find a perfectly valid and fulfilling religion without Jesus Christ or the church.[56]

But They Are Still Bad!

Regardless of these image-building endeavors, the facts seem to reveal that the majority of contemporary witchcraft expressions reflect the negative characteristics which we have seen in witchcraft history. These expressions are more in line with the thinking of the infamous Marquis de Sade, who teaches that the end of man is the satisfaction of all lusts—not the glory of God. The characters in his novels dissipate themselves in perverted lusts behind high walls and castles. It is noteworthy that, in recent years, his writings have had wide circulation.[57] They have especially influenced the contemporary "Theater of the Absurd." The German philosopher, Nietzsche, is in the same tradition. It is not surprising that Adolf Hitler found inspiration in these writers.

A Parody of True Christianity

In most of its forms, magic and witchcraft seek to parody and mimic Christianity. In its ceremonies, magic and witchcraft often use the invocation—to Satan. The charm utilized is the counterpart of the Bible. The witch services employ the Christian symbols such as the laying on of hands and kneeling. Fetishes are used to correspond to the elements of the Lord's Supper. Magical books bearing the name of Moses are used.[58] Instead of building up, however, the magic ceremonies tend to weaken faith in God and impair the emotions and the body.[59]

It is not enough, however, to study the origin, development, and extent of witchcraft and magic. How is a person to evaluate these remarkable, and in many cases reprehensible developments? Chapter three will discuss representative ways of explanation and evaluation and elaborate on lessons to be learned.

Chapter Three

HOW CAN I EVALUATE
WITCHCRAFT AND MAGIC?

From an historical perspective, at least three basic explanations concerning magic and witchcraft have been suggested.

First, there are those who advocate the severely rationalist view. This view teaches that witchcraft is a kind of mass hysteria, arising from psychological or sociological causes.[1] With the rise of rationalism and disbelief in a personal God, there came a corresponding disbelief in his opposite, the devil. Hughes contends that, by the middle of the eighteenth century, comparatively few educated people in Western Europe believed with any profound conviction, in either a personal God or a personal devil (John Wesley was an exception). Witchcraft was seen as priestly bunkum. Witches were seen as hysterical crones. By 1840, *Nuttall's Dictionary* dismissed witchcraft as a kind of pretended magic in which our ancestors believed. This is the no-nonsense, "pack-o-lies" school.[2]

Numerous people continue to hold the rationalist-psychological view. It should not be denied that psychological and sociological theories can help us understand and explain the occurrence of witchcraft and magic in society. There seems to be a connection in past history, as well as in the present, between abnormal psychological profiles and a turning to occult practices. For example, many witches have been sexually repressed persons. The sexual-repression view of witchcraft, however, like the statement that the deeply religious medieval nuns talked of Jesus in an almost fanatical way primarily because of sexual repression, is only a half-truth. Huxley has exploited this theory to its fullest in his famous book, *The Devils of Loudun.* Sigmund Freud once confessed to his friend Carl Jung that he felt obligated to make a dogma out of his sexual theory because he saw this as the "only bulwark of reason against a possible outburst of the black flood of occultism." [3]

Projecting Psychological Anxieties?

Another prominent rationalist theory states that witches are psychological projections created for the purpose of putting into concrete form deep anxieties. Anthropologists, such as Kluckholn and Howells, teach that witch-beliefs serve as an outlet for repressed hostility.[4] Geoffrey Parrinder suggests that a dramatic increase in witchcraft, and its inevitable persecution, is an outgrowth of tensions and stresses. These tensions are caused by sudden changes in values, customs, and technology. Such pressures invite the selection of a scapegoat.[5] This view is similar to Authur Miller's theory in his play *The Crucible.* Miller, of course, was also attacking the McCarthy anti-Communist scapegoat hysteria. Howells states that witchcraft is, at least, a less dangerous fantasy than the one which the Germans had concerning the Jews.[6]

Others say that witchcraft is an effective alternative to madness.[7] For Evans-Pritchard, witchcraft is functional in that it explains unfortunate events and circumstances such as those experienced by the Puritans.[8]

Some sociologists suggest, that in a democratic society like the United States, where social institutions do not demand absolute obedience, the individual feels isolated and insecure. He thus turns to witchcraft as one option in his quest for meaning and security. Others see witchcraft and magic rooted in man's need to be effective and get or exert power.[9]

A Genuine Religious Cult?

A second basic view concerning witchcraft and magic is the one suggested by anthropologists such as Margaret Murray. According to this view, witchcraft is to be seen as a genuine religious cult, the remnant of an extensive fertility belief. European witchcraft is a development out of the old pagan fertility religion of Western Europe.[10] American witchcraft has its primary roots in the European tradition.

Technical scholars have questioned this second basic view concerning witchcraft, first put forward by Margaret Murray in 1921. Men like E. O. James and Geoffrey Parrinder contend that she has overstated her case. There is not enough evidence, they suggest, to state that a clearly defined witch sect existed in Europe, in a continuous form, in the early centuries of the Christian era.[11] For Kelly, a more likely explanation is that the new cult of witchcraft resulted from a combination of folk memories, superstitions, and heretical practices.

It does not appear as an organized cult until the fifteenth century.[12]

Theory Three: The Work of the Devil

The third basic view concerning the origin of witchcraft has been stated in both extreme and moderate forms. This is the view of the medieval Catholic church and to a large extent the modern Catholic church. It is almost simplistic in nature. It has a great appeal for the modern Jesus Movement. It teaches that the devil is real, and that witchcraft and magic (especially black magic) represent demonic and satanic activity.[13] Although stated in different ways, most Fundamentalists and many conservative Protestants hold this view. It should be noted that this view does not necessarily negate important insights taught in the other two views.

Thus we have before us three basic explanations of magic and witchcraft: *1. The rationalist-psychological view, 2. The fertility cult view, and 3. The conservative-biblical view.* From the third perspective, the conservative-biblical view, magic, in its most ultimate form, came into being with the spiritual fall of man. Genesis 1:28 notes that God commanded man to master earth's potentialities in dependence upon God and in accordance with God's will. Satan offered man a knowledge and power contrary to God's will (Gen. 3:5). The desire and drive for knowledge and power in opposition to the command and will of God constitutes the essence of magic.[14]

Man, in approving Satan's proposal, chose to disobey God. In his desire for knowledge and power, he became God's rival. Magic is thus at its roots a rebellion against God. Man aligned himself with Satan and his demons.

Man enlisted their help in his search for knowledge and
power.

Not for the Christian

To see magic, as it is practiced in the world today,
as a gift of God, is to show ignorance of the basic teaching of the Bible. A Christian bends to God's will—he
does not seek to bend God's will or power to his.

Magic and witchcraft, from a conservative-biblical
perspective, can thus be seen as playing a part in Satan's world-wide rebellion against God and Christ.
Through magic, Koch contends that Satan attacks animals and men and everything in the material world.
Koch illustrates his understanding of the biblical teaching by experiences from his extensive counseling and
pastoral ministry in Europe. Specific examples are
given by Koch of how black magic is utilized in inflicting diseases on men and animals.[15]

Betty Smith's illustrations of satanic activity come
mostly from the current college scene. She tells of a
black warlock (male witch) in Miami, Florida, who in-
flicted illnesses on the boy friends of girls he wanted to
date.[16]

"Hate" Magic

The reality of hate magic is widely held today. According to Smith, a black witch hovered over the recent Broadway musical, *Celebration,* and caused
several disasters at the start. Cindi, a white witch, coun-
teracted with white magic and, after a month, the show
began to be relieved of disasters.[17]

Persecution magic, according to Koch, is utilized extensively in parts of rural Europe to milk the cattle of

an enemy dry. Casting spells is used by some magicians as if it were a sport, while others use it to further their own interests.[18] Interest in the power of the human eye is widespread. "Fascination" and "charisma" are terms used in relation to powerful eyes.[19] A dynamic speaker has always been known as a "spellbinder"; have you noticed the eyes of Paul Harvey as he speaks each night on television? [Example only; no personal reflection intended.]

In magical lore, a spell is produced by the release of demonic power through hypnosis, magnetism, mesmerism and extra-sensory influence.[20] Anton LaVey, head of the Church of Satan, is known for his hypnotic eyes. The girls in the California Manson family, who were arrested in connection with the Tate murder, said that Manson had cast a spell over them. He mesmerized them with his fervid eyes. P. K. Wrigley, owner of the Chicago Cubs in the 1930's, hired an "evil eye" to go out and cast a "whammy" on the opposing team in each game. The "evil eye" would sit behind home plate. Whether in jest or in earnest, there are those who claim witchcraft could be used today.[21]

Love charms for getting a man are used extensively among young people today. If you will press the tail feather of a rooster into your intended's hand, you will gain his love. At least this is what you are told in popular handbooks on magic.[22] A sixteen-year-old girl in New York walks around an unresponsive lover's home sprinkling salt over her shoulder at each step.[23]

Love Charms for Older Men

Smith, in her book *Today's Witches,* records numerous examples of young women who fall for older men as a result of the use by these men of a love charm. This charm is created by mixing three hairs from the girl's head with five from the man's head in virgin beeswax. After the spells are broken, the girls cannot understand why they could possibly have been attracted to these older men.[24]

Louise Huebner, a self-proclaimed California witch, has a monthly radio show in which she casts spells. She also casts spells at the Hollywood Bowl and on college campuses throughout the United States in the name of love and sexual vitality.

The techniques of removing spells is also attracting extensive interest among young people today. Louise Heubner has cut a record which includes a spell which can be used to get rid of an unwanted lover. Success incense is widely used. Charms for protection have now become a major business in the United States—expecially among young people in the counter-culture.[25]

"Death" Magic

One of the darkest areas that exists in occultism is known as death magic. This type of magic is practiced not only in the so-called primitive countries but in theoretically more civilized Europe and America. Koch tells of a woman in Europe who engages in black magic through the utilization of the magical books known as *The Sixth and Seventh Books of Moses.* She boasts that she has done away with her husband and daughters through inflicting diseases on them. She states that she was driven to inflict these catastrophes by the devil.[26]

A former professor at Columbia University became convinced that a man had done him a great injury. The enemy, a man in good health, in a very short time, died

of a heart attack. The professor had sat before his enemy's photo for hours, concentrating on his desire for his
death.[27] Black magic experts in Europe are reported
to kill so many cows and pigs that so-called "stable
magic" is widely feared.[28]

Even if these examples cannot be empirically proved
as due to black magic, their existence implies that our
culture is at a very low level. Some type of evil force
is abroad!

Forbidden by the Bible

After noting these examples of the harmful effects of
magic, it is not surprising to find that the Bible teaches
that magic and sorcery are offensive to God and related
to demonic forces. They are not to be seen as harmless
games to be experimented with as a stimulant for jaded
metaphysical appetites.

In the light of the danger of witches to the moral life
and redemptive purposes of God's chosen people, Ex-
odus 22:18 records that Israel was not to allow them to
live. Deuteronomy 18:10–12 states that sorcerers and
wizards are offensive to God. Obviously, black magic
and witchcraft were widely practiced in a degrading
way in Canaan as evidenced by the inscriptions found
on the Ras Shamra tablets.[29]

Jezebel, the wicked queen of the Northern Kingdom
of Israel, was deeply involved in witchcraft (2 Kings
9:22). Joram suggested that there could be no peace in
Israel as long as her magical practices prevailed. King
Manasseh of Judah practiced magical sorcery (2 Chronicles 33:6), and God called these deeds "abominations"
and stated that Manasseh had done wrong (2 Kings
21:11). Manasseh evidently followed in the steps of

Solomon, who according to tradition was a sorcerer.
Manasseh went so far as to sacrifice his own children
to the pagan god Moloch in the Valley of Hinnon. He
also practiced astrological divination, consulted magicians, and summoned the dead (2 Kings 21:6; 2 Chronicles 33:6). Perhaps Manasseh thought that he was
practicing a bit of practical ecumenism in the midst of
the multiplex "old religions" of the ancient Near East.
To the prophets, however, he was in league with Satan
himself—a very devil in human form. Judah and the
king suffered for these practices (2 Kings 21:10–16).[30]

Isaiah was paramount among the prophets of Israel
in his distaste for magic and witchcraft. He used savage
satire to attack them (Isa. 47:12–13). Jeremiah warned
Judah not to trust occultic leaders (Jer. 27:9–10). Babylon, an important home of magic, was destroyed by the
Persian ruler, Cyrus, who acted as a rod of God's anger
and purpose (Isa. 47:9). For Malachi, a part of God's
judgment on Israel will be a swift witness against witchcraft (Mal. 3:5).[31]

In the New Testament, Simon of Samaria saw the
superiority of God's power to his magical arts (Acts
8:13). In each of Paul's missionary journeys, he had to
confront satanic magical powers. Paul told Bar-Jesus, a
Jewish magician, that he was a child of the devil and
perverting the right ways of God (Acts 13:10). At
Ephesus, many Christian converts had engaged in
magical practices before their conversion. They burned
their books (apparently instruction books in magical
arts) after their conversion (Acts 19:19).[32]

In Galatians 5:20, witchcraft, or sorcery, or the giving
of magical potions, is listed among the works of the
flesh. Revelation 9:21, Galatians 5:20, and the other

references already mentioned, indicate that the Bible considers magic and witchcraft as serious transgressions of God's will. It is clear that sorcerers will have no part in the New Jerusalem (Rev. 22:15).[33]

An Apostasy of the End Time

Conservative authors, such as Unger, see witchcraft and magic as an important part of the gigantic apostasy of the end time which demonic forces are engineering. Unger interprets these apostate occult happenings as indications that history is rapidly moving toward a culmination point in the rise of the Antichrist. According to this view, the rise of the final Antichrist will be accompanied by the greatest demonstration of demonic wonders the world has ever seen (2 Thes. 2:8–10; Rev. 13:13,14). For Unger, witchcraft and magic are a part of a demon-inspired campaign which will issue in Armageddon. They represent Satan's attempt to take over the earth and banish the name of God and his Christ from this planet (Rev. 16:13,14). Christ's triumphant return, however, will smash Satan's plan and result in the defeat of Satan and his demons (Rev. 20:1–3, 10–15).[34]

A more mediating position is that of H. Richard Neff, as described in his recent book, *Psychic Phenomena and Religion.* He thinks that it is important to make a distinction between legitimate research in parapsychology and extrasensory perception and evil practices such as black magic and witchcraft.[35]

Neff would agree with Unger that psychic phenomena do occur. He would also agree that these experiences are often the instruments which the devil uses to entice people into false beliefs and wrong religious practices. The devil, as the master of deceit, uses true information to entice people and make them devotees of the occult. Then, when the people are "hooked," he moves in to destroy them.[36]

Both Neff and Unger agree that the Bible warns against magic and witchcraft. Both agree that this biblical warning should be taken seriously. They are convinced that numerous people, claiming to have psychic gifts, are fraudulent—and clever in their deceit. Furthermore, both authors would agree that many people have been harmed by occult practices. We have already described a number of examples of harmful spells and persecution magic.[37]

Neff would emphasize, however, that experimental work in parapsychology should be encouraged. To say that it is all evil is an over-simplistic answer to a complex problem.[38] Perhaps Unger would agree to a limited extent. His main emphasis, however, is on the danger of *any* liaison with the occult. For him, the occult is one of Satan's chief instruments of deception.

Do Evil Forces Seek Us Out?

A more philosophical, yet equally positive, conclusion is the one reached by the well-known scholar, Emile Cailliet, for many years professor at Princeton. He has had extensive experience with the occult, magic and witchcraft in Madagascar, Europe and the United States. Cailliet states that he believes that there are personal evil forces in the universe constantly seeking to graft themselves on us, if given the slightest opening. Like parasites, these evil forces seek to feed on our substance. They present themselves, at first, as innocent and harmless. If we yield to them, however, they become our masters and hurt us and those around us.[39]

Satan is the organizing power of these forces, affirms Cailliet. In the words of Peter, he is like a roaring lion, seeking whom he may devour. Cailliet's experience suggests that occult practices, such as magic and witchcraft, constitute the surest way to give ourselves to Satan. In these occult practices, the Evil One is often hiding behind false appearances.[40]

Granted the validity of the ultimate biblical appraisal of magic and witchcraft, there is an additional question which haunts many of us. Why, from a secondary and human perspective, would enlightened people, especially educated young people, revert back into magic and witchcraft? As we have seen, magic and witchcraft are probably pre-historical and certainly pre-critical and pre-Christian religious forms.[41] Let us agree that there is much that is fraudulent and evil about the occult. Beyond this, however, there is obviously a spiritual hunger which drives many people, both young and old, to search for wisdom and experience in the occult world.[42]

A Good Reaction to the Damaging Evil?

Modern occultism, especially magic and witchcraft, will damage many people, spiritually, psychologically and even physically. It is possible, however, that occultism will have the positive value of forcing our traditional churches and dominant culture to examine themselves and see their deficiencies. Perhaps it will cause the churches to create new and more dynamic life-styles and options.[43]

Many people, especially the young, have not seen Christianity as a personal, liberating force. The services of many of our churches seem dull, dusty and ossified. Along comes witchcraft as an imaginative and mysterious option. There is festivity and an awesome ceremony. Many are succumbing!

Jean Stafford, writing in *McCall's Magazine,* suggests that the Christian God is on vacation for many young people. But the need for Him was great on the part of many of the girls in the Manson family—Susan and Linda and Katie and Mary. With no true God, they created a blasphemous substitute in the person of Charles Manson of Southern California.[44]

Unfortunately, Christianity has become too closely identified with rationalism and the technocratic, scientific establishment. Led by Huxley, Heidegger, Heard, Leary, and others, many people have come to believe that Western man needs to return, with conscious effort, to a more primitive, non-rational state. Heidegger has turned to the poets of the Black Forest of Germany—Rilke and Holderlin. Huxley and Heard have turned to yoga and the mystery religions. Timothy Leary has turned to the Eastern religions and drugs. Others have turned to Zen Buddhism.[45]

In their search, some see witchcraft as a system which carries on a fight against the materialism and oppressive technocracy of the West. Witchcraft appears to bring them back to nature and mystery and magic.[46]

The search is on in the United States and the world for a messiah or messianic deliverance, and some have found their answer, at least temporarily, in witchcraft and magic. As already indicated, the witchcraft cult also serves as a vehicle by which its members can vent their frustrations against the society in which they find themselves.[47]

A Thing of Our Cities

Witchcraft's strength and growth are found primarily in the sprawling and impersonal metropolitan centers. It is in the city that people are being pulled apart by "future shock." They are being thrust into the Twenty-first Century while still unable to cope with the difficulties of the Nineteenth. The organized churches do not seem to have helped some people, especially youth, to cope with technological overdevelopment. Hunger for meaning has driven many back to forms of ancient pagan religions. And, as we have seen, witchcraft and magic are related to man's oldest religions. In this primitive religion, a frightening number see something to give meaning.[48]

For the person who has visited the so-called primitive countries which are still dominated to a large extent by magic and witchcraft, the idea of reversion to pre-Christian conditions is unthinkable. Fellinni's movie of pre-Christian Rome, *Satyricon,* shocks us with its portrayal of what the pre-Christian world was and is and could be again. We remember, from our studies, the moral schizophrenia and confusion brought on in ancient Greece and Rome by the moral inconsistency of their many gods and spirits. There was no fundamental and unified moral basis for the conduct of life.[49]

Witchcraft tends to be past-oriented and surely stultifies progress. The leaders of witchcraft are often clever, but as a group they are too unstable for long-range constructive leadership. This ancient religion or cult leads to a life characterized by a constant fear of witches and black magic. It is difficult to overstate the terror and fear that haunts the life of people in animistic countries. Hundreds of thousands of people spend their lives in conscious fear of being ravaged by witches and evil spirits.[50] If modern day devotees of witchcraft followed out all of the implications of their teachings, there would be a frightful relapse into darkness. The residue of Christian teaching in their subconscious is more valuable than they realize.

Within the Christian message, there is plenty of what people really seek and need. In Christ, and the Indwelling Spirit, God is not distant, unseen, and uncaring. Perhaps we should emulate again the mysticism and ecstasy which the early church found in the good news of the gospel. Christianity is a religion of color, fragrance, and melody. It is a religion of affirmation and celebration. The church provides a social unit based around love, acceptance, fulfilment, common service, and worship. Here is a basis for a real sense of community.

Christ Frees Us from the Power of Evil

Insofar as we are conformed to Christ, rather than being ruled by the spirit of this world, we are freed from the power of curses and evil spirits and fate. An authentic Christian does not live in an irresponsible spirit world, but in a world undergirded by a loving Heavenly Father. "For this purpose was the Son of God manifested, that he might destroy the works of the devil" (1 John 3:8). Christ "has delivered us from the power of darkness" (Col. 1:13). We need to celebrate again and again this freedom from fear and the shackles of fate. There is much that Christians can learn from the history of witchcraft, magic, and the occult. Among other things, this history tells us that we need to cut away the brush, using drastic pruning if necessary, to allow people to see what authentic Christianity has to offer.[51]

Gustave Flaubert has written a charming page about the humble village churches he knew as a lad in Europe. On stormy days two kinds of beings came into the churches for refuge. First, there were the birds, seeking protection from the storm. Second, there were men, seeking security in the presence of demonic forces which had become unchained.

As we have already seen, in our day, spiritual seeking on the part of countless people is perhaps greater than many of us realize. Perhaps there is a new day coming —before the consummation—when people will listen and come in. In the Revelation, John tells us that he saw red and black and pale horses galloping over the earth. These horses symbolize war, famine, and pestilence. But he also saw a white horse. For many scholars this horse symbolizes an effective proclamation of and reception of the gospel. Let us open the doors of our churches and share our faith concerning the victory that is available in Christ over the demonic powers.

Chapter Four

IS DEMON SUBJECTION
AND POSSESSION
REAL TODAY?

Interest in demon subjection and possession are part of the contemporary religious and occult revolution. Despite the fact that theologians—from Wreimarius in the Eighteenth Century up to Bultmann in the Twentieth Century—have refused to tolerate demons, belief in demons continues. An increasing number of people seem to accept demons and reject some theologians. In America, England, and France, demon possession is reported on the increase. And certainly in Latin America, the Indies, and Africa, it is as common as ever.[1]

Reports of demonic influence and possession flow in from dozens of sources. Foreign mission boards in the United States continue to receive reports of such demonic activity. An exhaustive study of demon possession in China by J. L. Nevius is based on dozens of questionnaires sent to missionaries and Chinese Christians before the Communist take-over. Nevius concludes that demon possession is what the name suggests. It cannot be equated with ordinary physical or psychological derangements. Similar reports have poured in from Korea, Indonesia, Africa, and South America.[2]

In recent years, home mission boards report a high incidence of demon possession in the United States. M. T. Starkes, a representative of a Baptist agency, tells of interviewing more than twenty persons who claim to have been demon possessed.[3] Christian workers in California state that they have had to study demon possession in order to minister to the "hip" culture. They report that hundreds of California young people are demonized. Drugs and occult practices, such as black magic, seances, and fortune telling have evidently been a "springboard" for the increase of interest in demon possession.[4]

Most of us have come into contact with people who have abnormal mental characteristics and whose behavior pattern is rather repulsive. It is sometimes hard to evaluate these people. Those who are trained in psychology usually suggest that the person's problems can be explained quite adequately by reference either to depth psychology or psychopathology.[5] To mention the word "demons" in some psychological circles is to be classified as being slightly abnormal yourself. In reaction to the psychological approach, some conservative Christians suggest that the demonic is lurking behind all abnormal phenomena connected with the emotional and spiritual life of a person.[6]

Jesus Believed Demons Were Real

When we turn to the New Testament, we discover that every facet of the life and ministry of Jesus was dominated by his belief in the reality of demonic forces.

Mark, probably the oldest Gospel, clearly reflects Jesus' total concern with the defeat of demonic powers. The demonic is closely related to the miracles of Jesus and his preaching. "If it is by the Spirit of God that I cast out demons, then the Kingdom of God has come upon you" (Luke 11:20). Evil for Jesus is not exhausted when one speaks of existential bad intentions.[7]

The driving out of demons was an important part of the early period of Jesus' messianic activity. At the very outset of his ministry in Capernaum, Jesus exorcised the demons from a possessed man (Mark 1:27). His disciples were also given the power to drive out demons (Matt. 10:8, Luke 10:17).

The importance that driving out demons (exorcism) plays in Christ's ministry has been a stumbling block to many who do not accept the reality of the supernatural world. Interpreters have explained demon subjection and possession and demonic exorcism in a number of ways.

Some scholars admit that Jesus appears to have believed in Satan and demons. For them, however, this belief represents a mere adaptation to the concepts of the age. It in no way represents the content of Jesus' teachings. Jesus' purpose was ethical, and he used the concepts of his time as symbols to serve ethical ends. This is sometimes called the accommodation theory.[8]

A second interpretation is similar to the first theory. It suggests that Jesus was a child of his day and was mistaken in his belief about demons. What the ancients call demon possession is today called mental illness. If this view is accepted, it raises serious problems. For Jesus, the casting out of demons was at the heart of his mission. This view is called the psychopathological theory.[9]

George Ladd suggests that there is only one interpretation which does full justice to the gospel data and to the integrity of Christ's person. This is the view which accepts the existence of demons and demonic possession as an objective reality. It is true that the ancient world at large believed in demon possession. There are distinct differences, however, between the teaching of Jesus and Jewish literature. Jesus uses sobriety and restraint in talking of demons. The magical element is absent in Christ's ministry.[10]

For Jesus and his disciples, in most cases, normal physical illnesses were cured by the laying on of hands or anointing with oil. Cases of possession were usually cured by the word of command (Matt. 10:8, Mark 6:13, Luke 13:32). In only one place is demon possession identified with mental disease (Mark 5:15). The chief characteristic of demon possession appears to have been the control of the body of the possessed in an abnormal way.[11]

Paul Believed Demons Were Real

The apostle Paul and the other New Testament writers likewise assume the existence of Satan and his evil cohorts. For them, the evil angelic powers are not peripheral, but belong to the central content of the New Testament faith. James Kallas suggests that the tragedy of contemporary theology is that it has failed to accept the centrality of demonology and eschatology as found in the New Testament.[12]

As has already been indicated, these New Testament teachings have come alive in the light of contemporary demonic expressions. Youth workers report that the only model which will enable them to understand the demonic expressions found in the occult is the basic biblical model. Physicians and theologians, such as Lechler and Koch, describe cases which appear to parallel closely those of biblical times. These men contend that physicians and psychologists who have difficulty in regard to the diagnosis and treatment of demonic cases can be helped by biblical insights.[13]

In antiquity, no mental disturbance was seen as necessary to cause possession. Bodily disturbances were regarded as being due to demonic influences. The next development, in the religious Middle Ages, held that psychic disturbances were caused by demons. The third stage is constituted by the modern scientific conception that there is no demonic possession. That which was formerly called possession is now seen by many as a split manifestation and a compulsive process.[14]

A fourth development, however, contends that not all phenomena called possession can be explained by means of psychological and psychiatric explanations. This approach insists that a very important unexplainable residue remains, for which there is no psychological explanation. Men who hold this view suggest that we hold open the possibility of a transcendent power such as a supernatural being (or beings) operating in a person's life.[15]

Scholars Have Other Explanations

It must be said that scholars in the field of demon possession, such as T. K. Oesterreich, believe that much, if not most, of so-called demon subjection and possession can be explained in psychological or socio-

logical ways. For Oesterreich, many people tend to believe in demons, if their age and culture accept such
a view. Doctors or pastors, who believe in demons, have
a strong influence when they suggest such a belief to
the people. At times, the environment becomes in-
fected with the occult, and hysteria develops. Possession then becomes a kind of imitative neurosis. For
some, an *a priori* predisposition toward possession can
be aroused by a dream or a sickness.[16]

According to Oesterreich, the cure of possession is
closely related to the origin of possession. There must
be isolation from demonic infectors, and strong coun-
ter-suggestions to eliminate the concept of possession.[17]

Oesterreich believes that the primary cause of demon possession is an expanded compulsion complex. In
many cases, people have externalized their conflicts. In
other cases, people purposely seek to be controlled by
a spirit. But for Oesterreich there is only one basic ego.
As a scientist, however, he suspends any final judgment.
He cannot give a purely negative answer to the possibility of actual supernatural demon possession. Oesterreich's work, *Possession, Demonical and Other,* is well
documented with examples drawn from all ages and
countries.[18]

Although some psychologists overstate their case,
people who accept the Christian world-view should not
react in a negative way by minimizing medical find-
ings. For example, evidence has been advanced that
certain drugs can alter psychic aptitudes, such as clairvoyance. Miss Sally Beaucamp, who had four or five
separate forms of personality split, at first appearance
looked like a demon-possessed person. Dr. Morton

Prince, however, fused the states of her consciousness and effected a cure.[19]

Despite many breakthroughs by science, a number of scientists, such as Tischner and Moser, admit that a residue of data related to demon possession remains which cannot be explained by psychological or medical categories. There are facts in this area which will not be denied and which cannot be explained by scientific theories.[20]

Christian, Use Your Intellect

The Hebrew-Christian philosophy insists that God has given man intelligence, and he should use it (Gen. 1:28). A *premature* recourse to explanation by demonic intervention could involve a renouncing of intelligence and constitute a flight into the magical. Christians should not be too gullible and oversimplify problems. There should be no fear on the part of Christian people in regard to scientific research in the field of the demonic.[21]

On the other hand, scientific research should not arbitrarily rule out all supernatural realities even though some scientists refuse to accept the possibility of any form of demonic influence. There are various levels which should be taken into consideration as the demonic is considered. Reductionism should be avoided. Theologians and scientists should join in a cooperative approach.[22]

For the Christian, the ultimate testimony to the supernatural and the demonic is the testimony of the Bible itself. However, before any detailed consideration of the biblical teachings is given, it will be helpful to turn to a psychologist and a psychiatrist who give an indirect and a direct witness to the personal power of the demonic.[23]

Although T. K. Oesterreich suggests that most of that which is called demonic subjection and demonic possession can be explained psychologically, he does leave room for a supernatural explanation, such as that given in the Bible. For example, his extensive research indicates that typical marks of possession have been constant from the New Testament times until today. Furthermore, serious Christians, well anchored in their faith, have had a remarkable immunity to possession. It is noteworthy that a mark of a possessed person is his tendency to curse in a violent way at the mention of the name of Christ. Upon conversion to Christianity, the evidence indicates that formerly possessed persons become healed almost instantly.[24]

A report is made by Oesterreich of genuine exorcisms on the occasion of the presentation of the Christian gospel. Various cases of the translocation of possession complexes from possessed persons to other people are also reported. Possessed people are reported as speaking in strange voices. Young girls who are possessed display the strength of three to seven mature men. Possessed people also display prophetic, clairvoyant, and telepathic abilities, including the use of foreign languages which they have never had an opportunity to hear. If supernatural demonic powers are not accepted as the reason for these happenings, it is hard to explain this type of behaviour. There is a noteworthy parallel between these reports and the New Testament accounts of possession. For example, the connection of possession with clairvoyance is parallel to the New Testament story of Jesus and the demoniacs. The demoniacs immediately acknowledged Jesus as the Son of God (Mark 5:7 f).[25]

The Evils of Demonic Possession

A characteristic result of possession listed by Oester-reich is the destruction of psychic integrity. This de-struction is accompanied, however, by symptoms different from those seen in schizophrenics, manic depressives, and psychopaths. Another result of posses-sion is the sudden incidence of increased sexuality.[26] Oesterreich seeks to explain most of the occurrences related to demon possession listed above in psychologi-cal ways. For other scholars, however, the acceptance of the reality of supernatural demonic subjection and possession, as described in the Bible, furnishes an expla-nation at an even more profound level. The biblical approach illuminates much of the extensive empirical data on possession cases collected by Oesterreich and others.

Dr. Alfred Lechler, a German psychiatrist, gives his primary attention to psychiatric forms of mental illness. In some cases, however, he recognizes psychic dis-turbance which he believes is caused by demonic in-fluence. He suggests that, in some of his patients, demonic subjection and mental illness occur simultane-ously.[27]

It is not easy, however, for a Christian psychiatrist to speak out in this area, Lechler reports. Lechler suggests that he cannot dismiss demonism as much of psy-chiatry does. On the other hand, he cannot go along with some Christian people who label almost all cases of schizophrenia, epilepsy, mental depression, and senile dementia as symptoms of demonic subjection.

Lechler further suggests that it is important to distinguish between demon possession, influence by demons, and demonic deception. Possession is the more serious and less frequent occurrence. Possession, for Lechler, is not an outdated biblical report nor a theological invention, but a dreadful reality.[28]

The Marks of Demonic Possession

The marks of the New Testament descriptions of demon *possession* agree in a remarkable way with the following marks of possession reported in our day: the double voice, clairvoyance, paroxysms, extreme bodily strength, resistance to divine things, exorcism, and a complete cure after expulsion. When a person is under demonic *influence,* Lechler notes that less extreme but no less definite characteristics are typical. These include non-receptivity to divine things, religious doubt, inaptness for true knowledge of sin, inability to concentrate in Bible-reading and prayer, persistent lack of peace, inner unrest, temper bursts, blasphemy, depression, and suicidal thoughts. With these marks is joined the various compulsions toward drunkenness, sexual immorality, falsehood, theft, smoking, and drugs.[29]

Many people who are willing to accept the reality of demonic influence or subjection deny the possibility of demonic possession. Lechler points out, however, that the Bible recognizes both demonic influence *and* possession and distinguishes between them. For example, in John 13:2, we read that the devil influenced Judas Iscariot to betray Jesus. In John 13:27, we read, "Then after the sop, Satan entered into Judas." In his extensive practice, Lechler has found many people whose condition bears a striking resemblance to the recorded cases of possession in the Bible. The Bible explanation of their condition gives a more satisfactory explanation than alternative psychiatric or psychological explanations.[30]

The British theologian J. Stafford Wright contends that it makes sense to say that, if a man's spirit is not occupied by God, it may be used by another. If it is merely empty, the inner being of man will either be unorganized or organized around some inadequate center. Unpleasant complexes may develop as a natural consequence. Possession by a demon may intensify these symptoms and may also produce a flood of supernormal effects. The demon may seize on unpleasant personality groupings that are already forming and emerge as a new personality in the person.[31]

In 2 Timothy 2:26, Paul writes of men who have been ensnared by the devil and captured by him to do his will. In Luke 13:16, we read of a woman who had been bound by Satan for eighteen years.[32] Such biblical statements appear to be more and more true to contemporary experience.

Demonic Subjection, Not Possession

It must be stressed, however, that *possession,* at least among Western people, is a much rarer phenomenon than demonic *subjection.* In many instances of so-called possession, one is really only dealing with a severe case of demonic subjection or the effects of a mental illness.[33]

Lechler suggests a number of factors which he thinks help to cause demonic influence, subjection, and possession. If a person openly lives a life of sin and persistently resists the Spirit of God, he is open to Satan's attack. Blasphemy is a cry to the devil and often prepares the way for bondage. People already under demonic subjection can influence some other person negatively.[34]

It seems to be particularly easy for those who engage in occult practices to fall victim to demonic subjection. Such practices include visiting a fortune teller, inquiring of the dead through mediums, and reading books on sorcery and horoscopes. Above all, a conscious subscribing of oneself to the devil, with one's own blood, will often result in a terrible form of demonic subjection and oppression. The motive behind this surrender to Satan is usually the desire to have some special wish fulfilled—whether it be wealth or a desire to uncover the future. Kent Philpott affirms that demon subjection often comes as a result of the desire for power—material, spiritual, or sexual.[35]

Falling Under the Ban of the Devil

Frequently it is discovered that people whose parents or ancestors have practiced sorcery fall under the ban of the devil. Dark powers are often transferred to relatives or friends just before death. It may be some time later before the people involved become aware of their strange inheritance. In such cases, the possession is not necessarily preceded by a period of demonic subjection, but may be instantaneous.[36]

And so, in all these ways, either knowingly or unknowingly, man lays claim to the services of Satan. But Satan does not give his services free of charge. If a person turns to Satan for help, he binds him and brings him into subjection. More often than not, ominous symptoms appear in the person's emotional and mental life, betraying the terrible bondage.[37]

The interested Christian is obviously not content to stop with the statement made by some scientists that it is impossible to understand all of the possession symptoms. It is important to study the insights which the biblical revelation gives on the diagnosis and cure of possessed people. The Christian does not engage in this study merely because he is inquisitive or daring or different. Such a study is a part of his mandate to help people.[38]

The situation in regard to demon possession is somewhat analogous to the problem of the validity of the rational proofs for God. The rational arguments for God including design and first cause cannot give us conclusive proof for God's existence, but they can make belief in God more probable. In a similar way, science and reason cannot give us conclusive proof for the existence of demons, but they can give us indications or intimations which make this belief more probable.[39]

The hints and unexplained data provided by psychological and psychiatric studies, prepare the way for the biblical explanations. As indicated earlier, both Oesterreich and Lechler point out the constancy of the marks of possession for two thousand years. Even Jung's theory of the collective subconscious cannot explain this constancy. The biblical hypothesis of supernatural demonic powers does offer a viable explanation.[40]

A second indication of the reality of demonic forces is the close correlation between the beginnings of psychic disturbances and occult and demonic involvement. As occult involvement increases, there is an increase in psychic conflicts.[41]

Lashing Out Against God

Another hint that undergirds belief in demonic forces is the God-opposing repulsion developed by healthy persons who become involved in occultism. Such a person often displays bursts of fury, fits of anger, and blasphemous shouts. He frequently flings a Bible into a corner or fireplace. Any talk of Christ is repulsive to him. The suggestion that he become a Christian evokes determined resistance.[42]

Resistance against divine influence is a characteristic mark of possession in the New Testament. The possessed person usually begins to cry aloud in the presence of Jesus and resists his influence (Matt. 8:29, Mark 5:7, Luke 4:34).[43]

Closely related to resistance is the prevalence of paroxysms or convulsions on the part of the possessed person at the sight of a church or a crucifix. Such a person is unobtrusive and friendly until the religiously related object is seen. Similar reactions are seen in the New Testament accounts of possession and exorcism (Mark 1:26; Luke 4:35,41; Acts 8:7).[44]

Splintering of the Spiritual Personality

According to representative psychological studies, the destruction of psychic unity occurs through depersonalization and dissociation. The New Testament indicates that psychic unity is also broken by demon subjection. The symptoms of this subjection can be differentiated from mental illness. A frequent characteristic of demonic subjection is the fact that the possessed person desires faith in God, but at the same time he resists divine influences. He does not desire to hate

Christ and blaspheme God, and yet he persists in blasphemy. This is more than a compulsive neurosis. Symptoms in contemporary cases are parallel to those of the Gadarene demoniac as described in Mark 5. He desired help and yet persisted in resistance.[45]

Depth psychology seeks to explain telepathic and clairvoyant powers by reference to subconscious factors. These explanations fall short, however, in explaining how the possessed person has clairvoyant insight and mastery of the unknown contents of utterly strange languages. Current cases are similar to the case of the young girl who followed Paul and Silas at Philippi (Acts 16:16). Possessed persons in the New Testament had an almost clairvoyant insight into the significance of the Person of Jesus (Matt. 8:29; Mark 5:7; Luke 8:28).[46]

Fast Cure for the Possessed

Another indication of a demonic center of operation is the speedy cure that comes to possessed people after exorcism. Most psychological disturbances are hard to cure, and therapy sometimes extends over years. In contrast, demon possessed persons can often be speedily released and cured when the apostlic gospel is properly presented. In the New Testament, such speedy cures are often mentioned (Mark 1:39; 5:15; Luke 8:2, 32–39). Can a case that involves an "extensive complex of compulsive phenomena" (to quote Oesterreich) be cured by a command for the demon to depart in the name of Jesus Christ? [47]

Thus we have seen that psychological explanations have not adequately explained the behavior of possessed people—at least in an ultimate sense. Into this vacuum the Bible comes and furnishes an explanation.

This biblical explanation maintains that some of the destructive activities in the soul-life of man are caused by the powers that rebelled against the Creator, namely, Satan and his demons.[48]

The statement of Jesus, "If I by the finger of God cast out devils, then is the Kingdom of God come upon you" (Luke 11:20), makes sense of much that is happening today. Karl Barth suggests that the knowledge of the demonic is a question of the knowledge of Christ and his mission. Demonology must be deduced from the facts of the Christian gospel.[49]

In the Old Testament period, the Israelites taught that many things surprising and fascinating originated from powers other than God. In the New Testament a similar teaching is found. Satan has the passion and the knowledge of a renegade, and so he often performs miracles which resemble those of Christ (Matt. 24:24; Mark 13:22; 2 Thess. 2:9; Rev. 13:13; 16:14; 19:20).[50]

The Armies of the Dark Powers

Thus the battle between Christ and Satan unveils the existence, essence, and authority of the dark powers. Displays of power, such as signs and wonders, are given by both Christ and Satan. It is therefore imperative to "try the spirits whether they be of God" (1 John 4:1).[51]

We are still standing in the interim between the dawning of the kingly rule of God in Christ's first coming and the final manifestation of God's kingdom in the second coming of Christ. In demon subjection and possession we see a continuing battle between God's lordship and the powers of darkness.

In spite of all his violent assaults, Satan has been vanquished. He can only engage in a rear guard action. In the battle against Satan there should be no thought of compromise. The goal is the total defeat of Satan. Since occultism is closely related to Satan's activity, it should be avoided. It has no place in the Christian world-view and life style.[52]

The chief concern and purpose of the Christians is that people under demonic subjection and possession should be liberated. As has already been indicated, Christian leaders are eager to accept all of the help that the scientific disciplines can contribute to this goal. The medical field helps when its research indicates the close relationship between the body and the mind. If they are divided, problems develop.[53]

Psychology and parapsychology point out that psychic dissociations (splits) arise out of a division in the subconscious. There is obviously truth in the insight that problems arise when the subconscious is activated through various suggestions received in a waking state.[54]

The Christian worker utilizes systematic observation and psychological tests. The work of Freud, Adler, and Jung indicates the importance of the personal and collective subconscious. Such studies also help in an understanding of the importance of dreams, repressions, and unresolved conflicts and tensions. In many ways such studies clarify passages such as Matthew 15:19, "out of the heart proceed evil thoughts . . ." and Romans 7:19, "the good that I would do, I do not." [55]

Modern Medical Advances Can be Helpful

Psychotherapy has done much to unlock the psychic connections and awaken unconscious conflicts, thus leading to solutions and release. If a person can be brought to face up to dangerous symptoms and helped to understand his conflicts, the hold of the demonic may be lessened. In fact, the Christian worker is especially careful not to diagnose certain cases as demonic subjection and possession without carefully investigating the background situation and excluding the possibility of pathological disturbance. This is important, for frequently people who are subject to possession characteristics are temperamentally sensitive and emotional. If such a person is told glibly that Satan has bound him or even possessed him, this statement can itself lead to much restlessness, fear, and depression. To further burden a person suffering from mental illness by telling him that he has fallen into the hands of the devil is inexcusable.[56]

In all doubtful cases, the Christian worker should refer to a Christian psychiatrist or counselor who has had experience in these matters. The Christian worker should also pray for the gift of discernment mentioned in 1 Corinthians 12. In the last analysis, it is only the Spirit of God who can help us see the plight of people and prevent us from making statements which are incorrect and harmful.[57]

Testimony of Kent Philpott

Kent Philpott, who works with hip youth in the San Francisco area, describes how he has had to pray earnestly for the spiritual gift of discernment as he works in difficult areas. Many of the young people with whom he deals are emotionally ill. But some are demon possessed, and Philpott states that there is a genuine recognizable difference between possession and mental illness.[58]

Our study reveals the importance of both psychological science and the Christian faith. These two disciplines should respect and acknowledge each other's God-ordained purpose. For example, Sigmund Freud, the famous psychologist, went beyond bounds when he taught that the religious content of faith is a neurosis-collect of humanity. And Carl Jung exceeded bounds in saying that all that which is called religious is the inner life projected to the outside. There should be mutual respect and the right kind of cooperation.[59]

Christians, and especially pastors, should have enough knowledge of neuroses and mental illness to know when to refer. On the other hand, Christians appreciate the statements of various scientists who affirm that the psychotherapeutic experience of change cannot displace Christian regeneration.[60]

You Must Have Christ

A person who accepts the normativity of the biblical revelation finds in the Bible a profound explanation of demon subjection and possession. The person involved has separated himself from God. Where God is despised, Satan enters. Man cannot remain in a vacuum, unoccupied. It follows that a Christian has the duty of pointing men to the facts of the gospel and undergirding the consequent liberation by accepting these people into a genuine Christian fellowship.[61]

Intensive spiritual activity is required to be effective in working with enslaved people. This type of work requires a sense of mission and a close relationship with the resources of the living Christ. Fanatics, extremists, and people with a sensitive nervous system are not consistently effective in work with demon-subjected or possessed people.[62]

As has already been suggested, it is highly desirable for the Christian worker to possess a combination of technical knowledge of psychological facts and Christian charisma (1 Cor. 2:10–15). The biblical description of the most effective worker is one whose life has the qualities of grace and outgoing and unselfish love.[63]

Basic Christian theology indicates that there should be admission of sin and confession as the first step in Christian conversion and liberation. This confession involves confession before God, and before a responsible Christian friend. There is also an important place for the congregational celebration of confession.[64]

Breaking the Bond with Beelzebub

An integral part of confession is a repudiation of Satan's dominion. As was true in earlier centuries, so it is today. Any compact with Satan must be consciously repudiated. Definite liberation can only come with such an act. Renunciation should be done before witnesses. There is to be a breaking with objects of sorcery (Acts 19:19). Contacts with the occult and friendships in the occult world must be broken.[65]

The Christian confessional culminates in absolution or the assurance of forgiveness (Eph. 1:7, 1 John 1:9). This is a decisive act in the attempt to help persons who are demon subjected or possessed. In the evangelical confessional, in contrast to that of the Roman Catholic, there are no conditions. The man subjected to demonic powers does not need a new yoke, but an unburdening. Of course, a hasty, premature absolution leads to false assurance and self-deception.[66]

As the Christian counselor reads such Scriptures as Romans 5:20, Ephesians 1:7; 1 John 1:7–9; 2:2, a very minute spark of faith begins to grow in the new convert. In the human-pastoral "your sins are forgiven you," the divine "you" of assurance is realized. If the person involved cannot accept forgiveness, then a probe for deeper causes is needed.[67]

As indicated earlier, resistance is usually a sign of demonic subjection. The Christian is to remember Jesus' words about prayer and fasting (Matt. 17:21), collective prayer (Matt. 19:19–20) and the laying on of hands with prayer (Mark 16:18, 1 Tim. 5:22, James 5: 14).[68]

The Power of Christ in Private

In definite cases of demonic possession, which are perhaps limited in number, exorcism or the expulsion of dark powers by the authority of Christ is utilized. To avoid the sensational, it should be done in seclusion. Lechler points out that this expulsion is often accompanied by screaming and mocking and cursing. In the New Testament, similar experiences accompanied exorcism. Kent Philpott of San Francisco reports that as an evil spirit left a possessed man, the expelled spirit knocked down a large man.[69]

Experienced leaders suggest that, after liberation, an important second step is the development of a dynamic spiritual resistance to all forms of evil. Consistent Bible study is basic. Fellowship in a dynamic Christian church is necessary (Acts 2:42, Heb. 10:25). To avoid any kind of relapse, the Christian life should include regular participation in the ordinances and a personal life of prayer.[70]

Can a Christian be possessed? Only God knows the heart of man. Some who profess to be Christians, have in reality never been converted. Perhaps the Christian is only obsessed, not possessed. It is also possible that, in order to cure a believer of pride or arrogance, God allows him to undergo a temporary period of possession. In 1 Corinthians 5:5, Paul tells of a believer being delivered up to Satan so he could be purged and ultimately saved for service. And believers do backslide! With genuine believers, if they are possessed, it is surely only a severe form of affliction and trial through which they have to temporarily pass.[71]

The New Testament is not primarily concerned with a detailed explanation of demonic enslavement or possession. Its main concern is with a proclamation of victory over subjection and possession through Jesus Christ. In our time, there is a fresh outbreak of the demonic. The Christian worker's main task is to confront this outbreak with the positive message of liberation. In reality, Satan and his demonic cohorts have been conquered by Jesus Christ. The announcement of this victory must be proclaimed and applied in a new and dynamic way in our time.[72]

Chapter Five

IS ASTROLOGY SATANIC?

For many people, astrology has become identified with goodness and peace—not with evil and the satanic. The highly successful Broadway musical *Hair* opens with a song which states that astrology has assured us that we are entering an era of peace and love. The ancient Babylonians believed that the planets and stars have a powerful influence on personal and national life. And now ancient Babylon's mystic beliefs are being taken up seriously or semi-seriously by the most scientifically sophisticated generation in history.

Harmless Fun and Games?

At first, thoughtful Christians looked at this astrological development as fun and games or the latest fad. Astrology provided a fascinating basis for conversation and discussion. Now, however, it is seen that astrology is becoming a religion or counter-religion for millions of people. Evidence is rising that it has serious negative effects.

When astrology becomes an alternative idolatrous

religion, an authentic Christian must stop and take no-
tice. Investigation reveals that from its beginnings astrology had a religious accent. The stars were seen as
equivalent to gods. The people in the First Century, for
example, felt themselves to be led, influenced, and
threatened by these planet-gods. Astrology belonged to
that which the Bible calls the fallen world system, or
cosmos, which is under the control of Satan and demonic spirits. Astrology was used by these invisible
world powers and rulers to trick, deceive, and warp
man, who is God's especially beloved creature (Ephes.
6:12). God warned his special people, Israel, to beware
of the danger of worshipping and serving the sun and
moon and stars (Deut. 4:19; 17:2–7).

Slaves of the Elemental Spirits?

The apostle Paul warned the Colossians not to allow
anyone to deceive them by making them a slave of the
elemental spirits of the universe (Col. 2:8). In the Epis-
tle to the Galatians, Paul reminded the Galatians that
they were formerly in bondage to spirits who are really
not gods (Gal. 4:8). But now that they have become
Christians and know the true God, Paul cannot understand how the Galatians can turn back to the weak and
beggarly elemental spirits, to whom they were once
slaves (Gal. 4:9).[1]

Scholars disagree on the exact meaning of Paul's reference to the "elemental spirits" in Colossians and
Galatians. This term probably refers to both the astrological worship of the stars and to the devotion of some
people of that time to Jewish legalism with its emphasis
on rules, rituals, and ceremonies (Gal. 4:10).

Historically, and today, astrology is related to the

worship of false gods and a turning away from the biblical God. The Second Commandment forbids Christian people from devoting themselves to anything in the heavens above which would take the place of devotion to the living God. It is from this biblical perspective that many Christian theologians today suggest that devotion to astrology opens the door to satanic invasion of personal and national life. Sybil Leek, a self-designated witch, affirms that astrology is her first love. She suggests that for her astrology and witchcraft have distinct links.[2] Obviously, astrology is closely related to the entire world of the occult, including its darker aspects, such as Satan worship, witchcraft, and black magic.

Why Does Modern Man Turn to "The Stars"?

From a historical perspective, it is evident that astrology has been identified with paganism. On many occasions, astrology has also been questioned from a scientific and rational standpoint. Before looking at the history of astrology and its basic ideas, it should be helpful to note the present-day extent of astrological involvement and some reasons why modern men turn to it.

Astrology claims that the planets and stars, both singly and in their various conjunctions, have a real, active and potent influence on human lives, and on world events in general. Some astrologers place more emphasis on predictions. Other believers in astrology prefer to emphasize its ability to diagnose character and assess an individual's potentialities.[3]

The Staggering Increase in Interest

The widespread interest in astrology is almost beyond description. For many, it is a fad which is fun and fascinating. For others it is worthy of serious study and the source of a substitute faith. In any case, it is no longer just a fad. It is now a phenomenon. Carroll Righter, the best-known American astrologer, has a by-line that is carried by 306 newspapers each day into some thirty million homes. Righter is only one of about 10,000 full-time and 175,000 part-time astrologers in the United States.[4]

Maurice Woodruff, prominent British astrologer, has sold more than twenty million copies of his two basic books on astrology. His newspaper column is syndicated around the world to newspapers with a combined circulation of over fifty million. He receives up to 5,000 letters a week from people seeking his advice.[5]

Time Pattern Research Institute programs a computerized horoscope on an IBM 360. You feed in the important data, and the machine reads out your horoscope. You can charge the $20.00 cost at your department store. A 10,000 word horoscope reading comes out in two minutes. An estimated 30,000 customers a month receive these "personalized" horoscopes. Emergency help is available, day or night, if you pay a monthly fee to an astrology company. One such company, Zodiatronics Telephone Service, provides computer horoscopes on 2,000 college campuses.[6]

Has "Woman's Lib" Heard About This?

It is estimated that 1,200 of the 1,750 daily newspapers in the United States carry daily horoscopes. There are about twenty magazines, many female in orientation, that deal mainly with astrology. Women astrological devotees outnumber men three to one. Supermarket and drugstore checkout counters have tiny "purse books" on astrology available.[7]

Television and radio have begun to fill more of their hours with astrologically "hip" disc jockeys and discussions of the occult. Maurice Woodruff, the English astrologer, makes his predictions during prime television time. "What's my Sign" is an astrology panel show.[8]

The fashion industry swims in astrology. Perhaps this trend is accelerated because movie and entertainment stars, opera singers and show people are "nuts on astrology." Investors consult astrologers. The advertising people are more and more using astrological motifs in advertisements.[9]

The radical "free colleges" for dropouts have large offerings in such courses as Advanced Astrology and Occult and Astrology Workshops. Beginning courses in astrology are offered in motel conference rooms across the nation and advertised widely in urban newspapers. Graduate master courses are also advertised. In England, such schools as the London Faculty of Astrological Studies awards diplomas to students who complete a two-year course.[10]

All the Way Around the World

Astrological interest is world-wide. In Britain about two-thirds of the people read horoscopes. Germany has at least eighteen million followers of astrology. In France, more than 650 million dollars annually is paid to astrologers and fortune tellers. Some 53 per cent of the French people read their horoscopes daily. One French astrology magazine has a circulation of 400,000.

In India, astrology retains her old position as Queen of the "sciences." Astrology permeates every sphere of Indian life. Madame Blavatsky, founder of Theosophy in 1875, obtained many of her ideas from Indian astrology. Astrology has ranked high in China for centuries. Mao-Tse-Tung officially disapproves of astrology, so it is underground in Red China now. In most other parts of the Far East it is still flourishing. Astrological flags are used in public processions in Vietnam and in other parts of what used to be Indochina. There is a 200,000 strong federation in Japan to which professional astrologers belong.[11]

The interest in astrology is obviously widespread. This leads to the question: Why?—at this particular time in history?

The Reasons They Give

One young lady reports that she has found a sense of oneness with the cosmos through astrology. Her experience in the Christian tradition had not given her a sense of cosmic unity or wholeness. Astrology made her feel that she was an important part of the whole big universe.[12]

In the young-oriented counter-culture, both astrology and ecology are popular. The reason is that both are based on a wholistic understanding of the interrelatedness of nature and man. People are yearning for a unity with the entire cosmos—both terrestial and celestial—in physical, mental, and spiritual ways.[13] McLuhan suggests that interest in astrology is rooted in youth's desire for psychic communal integration.[14]

To Satisfy Deeply-felt Needs

Other young people turn to astrology as a myth and symbol system, a substitute religion, that satisfies deeply felt needs. Modern behaviorist psychology is abstract and almost mechanical. It makes the universe seem unalive. The symbols of astrology seem more alive and dynamic. Scorpio is more concrete than the term "extrovert." [15]

Despite evidence to the contrary, many people find astrology, in its modern dress, a life-expanding and helpful force. One man reports that he finds in the stars signposts for his life and clues to his destiny. For this man, astrology helps to sort out life styles and furnish self-identity. It seems to provide personal integration.

Psychologist C. G. Jung had horoscopes cast for some of his patients. This horoscope work was not done in order to predict the patients' future, but to call attention to elements that might lie in their personality. The materials received from the horoscope could be used to provoke talk, invoke self-analysis, and perhaps create insight.[16] Jung's theory of the collective subconscious teaches that the stars cast psychic imprints on the soul of the individual.[17]

The Lack We Have Left

Traditional religious groups and technical science have obviously not satisfied the religious and psychological needs of many young people. In a world of uncertainty, people want help and meaning. In a similar time of uncertainty in Roman history, Rome turned to astrology. Today, young stargazers are responding to a similar case of disintegration and disenchantment.[18]

It is interesting and discouraging to note that among the most ardent astrologers are former practicing Catholics and conservative Protestants. Some of these people have dropped out of the "organized" church. Marc Edmund Jones, the dean of American astrologers, was a Presbyterian minister. Some astrologers, such as Carroll Righter and Jeane Dixon, seek to stay in Christian circles. Kerr contends that the resurrection of astrological belief from the graveyard of medieval superstition is an indictment of organized religion and the technological society.[19]

It is important for a person to have some knowledge of the history of astrology if he is to understand it and properly evaluate it. The literature is vast, but a few key events in the history of astrology will be noted.

The Babylonian Origins of Astrology

The actual beginnings of astrology are lost in the mists of time. By 2,000 B.C., when the Sumerians began writing in cuneiform, we know there was already a developed body of astrological doctrine. Western astrology comes primarily from Babylon. Enormous observatories called ziggurats were constructed, some over thirty stories high. On the top of these ziggurats, the priests studied the stars for clues to human destiny. These ziggurats were prototypes of the Tower of Babel (Gen. 11:1–10), which was an attempt to scale the very throne of heaven.[20]

The reason for such astrological studies by the ancients is easily recognizable. The influences of the sun on the earth and the moon on the seas were obvious. It was easy to believe that those other bright deities, the planets, which were always moving among the fixed stars, should be concerned with man's problems and destiny.[21]

The planets were identified with active gods and were thought to be actual superbeings. The characteristics of some of these planet-gods could be inferred from their appearance and movement. Mars was a red fiery wanderer and was the god of war. Mercury's quick motion near the sun gave it a nervous quality. Jupiter was big and bright and suggested power, success, and joviality. Bright-burning Venus, seen often in the evening, suggested love.[22]

The "Parade of the Animals"

The Zodiac is an observational construct. It was framed by tracing the path of the sun through the stars. The stars in the Zodiac belt do not form obvious patterns, but eventually the ancients discovered twelve such patterns. The twelve constellations of the Zodiac came from the number of moon cycles in the year. These twelve cycles comprise one circuit of the sun around its path (a year). The patterns discovered were imagined to be the outlines of animals of ancient legends. The word "Zodiac" means "the parade of animals."

The zodiacal sign, Gemini (the Twins), has a visible relation to two principal bright stars (Castor and Pollux). Scorpio is a grouping of fifteen stars resembling the stinging tail of that dangerous insect. Other signs do not have such an obvious grouping.[23]

As the planets wandered through the narrow belt of the Zodiac, they exhibited changes of mood. The earth was seen as the center of the universe. When the earth's motion made the other planets seem to slow down or reverse, the gods were thought to be irritated. The Sun rejoices in Leo (July 23—August 22) because it is summer and the king of beasts resembles him in strength. The sun is exalted in Aries (March 21—April 19) because Aries is a fiery sign associated with spring. The sun is in exile in winter's Capricorn (December 22—January 19) and in the autumnal Libra (September 23—October 23). The other planets have similar fluctuations of temperament.[24]

Scriptural Rejection of Astrology

The Jews were led by inspiration to reject this astrological development. The Lord God *created* the stars, planets, sun, and moon. They were not gods. Foreigner's observatories and their staffs were condemned outright. Isaiah and Ezekiel, among others, vigorously opposed astrology. Some astrological terms were used in Daniel and other biblical books, but they were modified and purged of their pagan connotations.[25]

The Egyptians developed a great center for astrology at Heliopolis, near modern Cairo. They emphasized personal prediction. India and China had extensive developments in astrology. There was a parallel but independent development of astrology in pre-Columbian Mexico and in the more southern lands of the Mayas and Incas.[26]

The conquests of Alexander the Great brought astrological wisdom to Greece. Aristotle supported it, and the mystery religions, such as the Pythagoreans, offered materials for adaptation.[27]

Hipparchus Programmed the "Houses"

It is from the Roman period that we get our present astrological system. Hipparchus (150 B.C.) more fully developed the Zodiac. He also formulated the twelve houses and identified them with mythological figures. Each segment of the Zodiac is called a house because it was thought that the gods lived in the heavenly bodies. The Alexandrian scholar, Ptolemy (A.D. 150) used the work of Hipparchus and systematized the doctrine of astrology. Ptolemy's system was used until the time of Copernicus in the Sixteenth Century.[28]

Copernicus Embarrasses the Astrologers

In the Sixteenth Century, Copernicus discovered that the sun instead of the earth was the center of our solar system. This meant that the planets do not move about the earth in circles. Astrologers, however, have continued to use the earth-centered view of Ptolemy. They have slipped two of the three planets discovered since 1781, Uranus and Neptune, into their tables of planetary influences. They have not bothered with Pluto.[29]

During the Middle Ages, Europe was gripped by astrology. University chairs for astrology were established. Luther rejected it and called it a "shabby art." [30]

With the coming of the Age of Rationalism (1750), astrology declined in influence. Astronomy and astrology finally parted company. But two world wars sparked a revival. We have already described the spectacular renewal of this pagan art or counter-religion in the last decade.[31]

As can be seen from its history, astrology is very complex. Although misunderstanding is often created by over-simplification, it should be helpful to set forth a few aspects of a simple horoscope.

Casting the Simplest Horoscope

The simplest horoscope is the birth chart. On such a chart the position of the solar system at the precise moment of the person's birth is considered important

and is therefore recorded. (Birth charts can also be prepared for countries—or corporations! They are handled
just as though the country, or corporation, were an
individual.)

Of first importance is the Zodiac sign the sun is in at
the person's birth. The sun sign is dominant because of
the historic importance attached to the sun. The basic
quality of each sun sign, as we saw in the historical
study, is derived from the mythology rather arbitrarily
associated with the names given to the signs by the
ancients.

Active sun signs include Cancer—the Crab (June
22—July 22); Aries—the Ram (March 21—April 19); Libra—the Scales (September 23—October 23); and
Capricorn—the Goat (December 22—January 19). Persons born under these signs are supposed to be active,
creative, and to conceive plans well.

Stable or fixed signs include Taurus—the Bull (April
20—May 20); Leo—the Lion (July 23—August 22); Scorpio—the Scorpion (October 24—November 21); and
Aquarius—the Waterman (January 20—February 18).
Those who bear these signs are positive and sustaining
personalities.

The remaining signs are mutable and variable: [32]
Gemini—the Twins (May 21—June 21); Virgo—the Virgin (August 23—September 22); Sagittarius—the
Archer (November 22—December 21); and Pisces—
the Fishes (February 19—March 20).

Just as important as is the sign into which one is born
is the sign of the Zodiac that was rising (ascending) in
the east at the exact time and place of birth. It is also
important to record the position of all other planets at
the moment of birth. A planet is powerful in some signs

and weak in others. Each sign has a ruling planet or planets. A planet is a strong force for good when it occupies its own sign. An example would be the planet Venus occupying the sun sign Taurus. A planet is weak when located in a sign opposite its own.[33]

Covering Almost Any Situation

Mercury and Venus hold special importance because they are closer to the sun. Mercury brings the influence of activity. Venus brings life and womanly sensitivity. Mars, God of War, indicates energy and strength. Jupiter expresses material well-being and expansion. Saturn is conservative. All such data gives the astrologer enough material to cover any kind of human problem.[34]

All charts consist of two parts. The first, as we have seen, is an outer ring showing the location of the signs of the Zodiac at birth. The second is an inner chart divided into twelve "Houses." Each House represents a different aspect of earthly life. For example, the first House concerns personal appearance. The second House has to do with finances. The ninth House deals with religion.

The positions of the signs of the Zodiac, and the planets among them, affect the Houses below. Even the angles between the planets are significant. If they are close they reinforce one another. If negative planets are in opposition (180° apart), they represent possible disaster.[35]

But There's More—Say the Astrologers

The factors enumerated are just a few of the hundreds that can enter into the preparation of a horoscope. It is an exacting process which follows definite rules and traditions. The brief astro-advice columns which give quick, slick answers are called "Slop astrology." The more extensive magazines are devoted to "Pop Astrology." Serious astrology is complicated and detailed.[36]

A man who was a Pisces (February 19—March 20) went for a private horoscope session. If the astrologer had told him the truth, he would probably have left offended. Astrologically speaking, Pisces is the weakest sign, and those who dwell in the Twelfth House reside in the loser's palace. A person under this sign is given to mental instability, poor health, and lack of control. The astrologer escaped her problem by stating that the man was born near another sign which meant good influences. She was able to weave the possibilities for a Piscean into a fairly constructive profile.[37]

How Does Astrology Work?

Is astrology more than intuition on the part of the astrologer and faith plus hope on the part of the one for whom the horoscope is cast? If so, then how does it work?

As we have noted, some sophisticated astrologers embrace Jung's idea of psychic footprints in each person's life. In recent days, the idea that some kind of emanations issue from heavenly bodies and affect a person's character and destiny has staged a comeback. Dr. Maki Takata affirms that the composition of human blood changes in relation to the eleven year sunspot cycle, to solar flares, and to sunrise. The new Cosmo-Biology attempts to join heredity and the stars.[38]

It is true that man is beginning a fresh study of the

effect of all forces—terrestial and celestial—on his life and well-being. But it does not seem likely that the gravitational force of the sun, moon, and stars can have any *direct* effect on such a small organism as an individual man.[39]

In the meantime, astrologers will go on teaching that particular planets influence particular facets of human personality or specific events. The possibility of so many variables and so much generalized language makes collective horoscopes possible. On a given day, Jeane Dixon told the Aries people that they would enjoy an unpressured Sunday. Take full advantage, she said. Join forces with friends at church and gatherings. This is a logical statement for a Sunday. It could hardly be disputed.[40]

Tell Them What They Want to Hear

The good astrologer senses the mood of his client, notes his problems, and finds the most positive way of fitting them into the context of the horoscope. Then he looks ahead and shapes predictions so that they amount to constructive counsel. All of us need a guide or a philosophy or a world-view. Some people seem to be satisfied with what they get in a horoscope.[41]

How can astrology be evaluated? There are at least three levels of evaluation: scientific, psychological, and theological.

Scientifically speaking, with the exception of some recent interest in Cosmo-Biology, already mentioned, there is little in ancient or modern astrology of merit.

Astrologers continue to base their calculations upon the descriptions of the universe as laid down by Ptol-

emy in A.D. 150. This view teaches that the earth is at
the center of the planetary and solar motions. Modern
sciences teaches that the earth is not the center of our
solar system—let alone the universe. In fact, there are
millions of solar systems—each one with planets revolv-
ing around its sun. Furthermore, the planets do not
move in circles, but in epicycles. Optical and radio tele-
scopes have shown us the true nature of our solar systems and the magnitude of our universe.[42]

Modern astronomy reveals a motion of the earth
which makes the whole apparatus of zodiacal signs rest
upon an illusion. The earth wobbles like an expiring
top, a phenomenon called the precession of the equi-
noxes. This precession affects the position of the sun on
a given day. The Ptolemy charts, still used by astrologers, are wrong.[43]

The Little Rays That Aren't There

The rays from the planets falling on a child at birth
are said to be decisive in his life. Actually, the planets
emit no light of their own. The source of light is found
in the fixed stars, while cosmic rays originate in the
Milky Way. The planets, like our earth, radiate neither
light nor cosmic rays.[44]

Astrological predictions often contradict themselves.
In Germany, three horoscopes were published just
before President J. F. Kennedy's death in November,
1963. One said he would be re-elected, another said he
would die, another said he would retire because of illness in the summer of 1964. When 500 astrologers
make their predictions, some of them will always approach the truth. The successful predictions are publi-
cized. What about the 490 false predictions? [45]

No Scientific Basis for Astrology

Kerr concludes that one may safely say that scientific premises for astrology do not exist. But this does not seem to upset its advocates. The reason, of course, is that most people do not follow astrology as a science. It has become a counter-religion in our time. This is why many evangelical Christians see it as having satanic characteristics.[46]

How is astrology to be evaluated from a psychological perspective? Some specific case histories may illustrate its dangers. A secretary, usually outgoing and alive, would withdraw completely on certain days. These days were not connected with the female cycle. The employer discovered that her horoscope pointed to troubles on those days, and so she lived in fear and withdrawal. Many other examples could be cited. Some people, for example, refuse to date Leos because they are "incompatible."[47]

According to Koch, a negative horoscope reading may have serious effects on a melancholic or fatalistic type of person. The reading will oftentimes sway him to a lethargic escape from responsibility.[48]

A woman who killed her son reported to the police that an astrologer had predicted that her son would never regain his full mental health. In order to save him from this terrible future, she killed him. The astrologer was not arraigned. The woman was sentenced to a long prison term.[49]

The "Self-Fulfilling Prophecy"

Psychologist Joyce Brothers criticizes astrology for creating "the self-fulfilling prophecy." Oftentimes saying a thing is going to happen will actually bring it about.[50] Mussolini was told that he was born with his sun in Leo. These two signs combined predicted that he would be filled with aggressive ambition and seek power. Scorpio was ascendant in Edgar Allen Poe's horoscope, and Poe was haunted by a morbid obsession with violence and death. Brigitte Bardot's sun-sign is Libra, ruled by Venus, the planet of love. Which was more important—the prediction or the actual practice—in the lives of these people?

A prominent German medical doctor and hospital superintendent recently issued a report on the dangers of astrology. His experiences reveal that in many cases astrology produced serious psychic disturbances, a fear of life, despair, and other disorders in sensitive people. Astrology tends to paralyze initiative and powers of judgment.[51]

From a theological perspective, a number of weaknesses have already been mentioned. Central to the Hebrew-Christian faith is the concept of God as the Creator. Jesus Christ is the exclusive mediator between God and man. The stars and planets are created objects—not persons made in the image of God.[52]

There is no evidence in the Bible that the stars, sun, and planets are meant to be signs and guides for men. The Bible clearly rejects pantheism (the idea that God and nature are one). Astrology so endangers the biblical faith that the Hebrews were instructed to take drastic measures and to rid themselves of any who worshipped the sun or moon or stars (Deut. 17:2–5).

The apostle Paul urged the Galatians not to put their trust in elemental spirits or beggarly elements. Upon being converted, the Christian believers at Ephesus burned their astrological books in a public ceremony. Paul points out to the Colossians that in Jesus Christ are hidden all the treasures of wisdom and knowledge (Col. 2:3).[53]

The Biblical Answer to Astrologers

A chief biblical emphasis is on the fact that man finds fulfilment in God's fellowship and service and not in self-will or Promethean pride. The followers of astrology seek to bind the heavenly powers to their own purposes instead of God's purposes. In this regard, they repeat the sin of Lucifer and can be called satanic.[54]

Although men inherit a proclivity toward evil from Adam, there is enough freedom left for responsibility before God. Man is not a puppet before God. God limited himself in giving men freedom. Astrology tends to emphasize that men are not free, but determined by cosmic forces.

The Bible gives the Christian assurance of victory over death, a resurrection body, and life in the New Heaven and the New Earth. However, there is to be no attempt to calculate a detailed future. In fact, the assurance of a glorious future, to be made real through God's power, is given primarily to help the Christian to live more dynamically and effectively in the present. Astrology violates clear biblical teaching in its attempts to predict details of the future (Matt. 24:36). In Dante's picture of the astrologers in hell, their heads are twisted so that they can only see backwards. This is their punishment for attempting to pry into the future which is the exclusive prerogative of God.[55]

An Incident Involving Satan?

As indicated earlier, astrology, as a part of the occult, has been in many instances the instrument of Satan in leading people into the slavery of fear and the despair of uncontrollable forces. Koch tells of a minister who paid an expensive fee to have a detailed horoscope cast for himself. He wanted to prove that astrology was a colossal fraud. To his astonishment the smallest details of the horoscope predictions came true. After eight years, he concluded that he had become the victim of demonic powers working through the horoscope. He renounced completely his connections with astrology. To his surprise he now observed that his horoscope was no longer correct. He is convinced that a person exposes himself to the possibility of satanic enslavement when he becomes actively involved in serious astrology.[56]

Despite the obvious scientific, psychological, and theological weaknesses, astrology is spreading like an epidemic in our day, even among church members. What is the dynamic that drives people to astrology in this "enlightened" period? Evidently the churches are not meeting some basic needs which astrology partially satisfies. People are seeking a sense of belonging in a universe that seems inhospitable and cold. They are looking for fulfilment and practical guidance in day-to-day living. They want the sense of self-identity and personal significance. They desire a sense of security in the midst of change.

Once again, people must hear the message that the God of Jesus Christ is the sovereign Creator. God is in charge. God still loves man and seeks to restore him without destroying his freedom. In the Son and the Spirit, the Father God can be known as personal and real. In Christ is found authentic freedom—not stifling slavery. In the Christian way is to be found creativity and joy.

The early Christians not only *out-thought,* but they *out-lived* and *out-died* the pagans. The growth of astrology indicates that we must set our Christian house in order. In the final analysis, the basic answer to astrology is for Christians to *be* authentic followers of Jesus Christ. "And I, if I be lifted up, will draw all men unto me." Christ has won the battle over occult and satanic powers. We must appropriate and incarnate the victory.

Chapter Six

CAN I HAVE
MY FUTURE INTERPRETED
AND PREDICTED?

In ancient times, divination (forecasting the future) was the queen of the occult arts. The very word "divination" indicates that this art professes to predict future things or reveal secret things by supernatural or divine means. During the early Christian centuries and the Middle Ages, divination was singled out for attack by Christian leaders. It continued to lose status, especially in the Nineteenth Century. In recent years, however, divination of various kinds, especially the ouija board, palmistry, and Tarot reading, has become an important part of the occult revolution.

As was seen in the chapter on astrology, possibly the earliest of all forms of prediction utilized the stars. Another popular method of divination among the Babylonians was reading the livers of animals. Archaeology has uncovered some 700 tablets which contain prophecies obtained through looking at the liver. Evidently the liver was seen as the seat of life and was easy to identify and remove.[1]

Babylonian kings depended on the study of the liver

to determine dates and the results of revolutions and wars. The Babylonian seer or priest would remove the liver from an animal and take it to the altar of the god who controlled the king's future. There the seer would check the liver's shape, convolutions, and arrangement of blood vessels for clues as to the dates and results of wars. If the seer was right in his predictions, he was honored. If the seer made a bad error, he usually lost his life.[2]

The Roman rulers were very much influenced by their official state diviners. The seers decided the days for wars by watching the flight of the birds, examining the entrails of animals, and watching lightning and thunder.

Crystal ball gazing or "scrying" was popular in the Middle Ages. The glass ball or a mirror helped the seer to enter into a trance. Whatever visions came to him in the trance, or whatever words he uttered, constituted the prophecy. Since the subconscious forces were removed from conscious control, the trance oftentimes provided entrance for demonic powers.[3]

In the contemporary period, many forms of divination have been revived. Two of the most popular are palmistry and Tarot cards.

Divination by Palmistry

Prediction by examining the shape of the hands and the lines on them—known as palmistry—is as old as civilization. The Romans said, "By the paw you know the man." Today, palmistry is a part of the occult revolution. Interest in the hand as an indication of personality trends is also being evidenced by physicians and law enforcers.

Palmistry teaches that the lines of our palms were impressed at birth by cosmic rays and consequently reveal our character. Palmistry follows the principle of "as above, so below." The reverse analogy is also true—from our hands we can tell our fate.[4]

"Chirognomy" studies the shape of the hands. Square palms and short fingers constitute the "Practical Hand" —heavy, coarse, slow, and primitive. The "Intuitive" or "Psychic Hand" has a long palm and short fingers. The "Sensitive Hand" has long fingers and a long palm. It is the artist's hand—for the keyboard or the paint brush or clay. Durer's "Praying Hands" represents the "Sensitive" Hand. The "Intellectual Hand" has a square palm and long fingers.[5]

"Chiromancy'" tells your future by the lines and mounts of the palm. The seer professes to be able to tell how long you will live by the measurement of your "Life Line." The Life Line begins at the middle of the side of the hand and turns toward the bottom. If you are to reach seventy, the Life Line should be high and strong and go to the thumb's base. The "Head Line" is across the middle of the hand. The longer the line, the better the head. Above it is the "Heart Line." If it begins near the first finger, it can indicate many loves. If the Heart Line begins between the second and third fingers, it may mean the person is cold. If it joins the Head Line—the heart rules the head. The "Line of Fate or Saturn"—up the middle—shows good or bad luck.[6]

Unfortunately, palmistry is often used for self-fulfiling fortune-telling. A young girl was told that her hand lines indicated that she would be murdered in her thirtieth year. She told her family that she had decided to

"live it up" since she would die so young. She drifted
into prostitution, had several abortions, and died at
twenty-four.[7] There may be some truth in the teaching
that a person's hand is correlated with his personality
traits. But to predict a person's future from physical
traits is dangerous and often self-fulfiling.

Closely related to palmistry is "Automatic Writing."
The basis for such writing is the theory that inner being
flows through the fingers. An outside control is said to
take over and guide the hand. It was in such a way,
reports W. B. Yeats, that his well-known work, *A Vision*, was dictated to his wife, Georgie.[8]

Divination by the Tarot Cards

The brutal murder of Dr. Victor Ohta and his family
in California in the Fall of 1970, involved the use of
Tarot cards. The incident focused attention on the
revival of ancient divination by Tarot.

Fortune telling with cards is an extremely old device.
The Romans were probably the first to employ the
method, the cards they used being in the form of small
wax tablets. Playing cards of the "pasteboard" type
evolved around A.D. 800. In Europe the earliest paper
cards were called Tarots, which means "tablets of fate."
Their origin, like that of cards in general, is shrouded
in the mists of antiquity.

Regardless of its source, Tarot became widespread in
Renaissance Europe, and the deck was eventually
standardized. The ancient seventy-eight-card Tarot
decks generally included fifty-six regular playing cards
known as the "Lesser Arcana." In addition to the fifty-
six cards, the Tarot deck contained twenty-two pic-
torial cards known as "trumps," the "Greater Arcana,"

or the "Major Arcana" cards, plus an unnumbered card known as the "Fool." Most people today are unaware that an ordinary pack of playing cards is a direct descendant of the Fourteenth Century Tarot deck.[9]

The twenty-two Major Arcana cards picture, in addition to the Fool, such symbols as the "Magician," the "High Priestess," the "World," the "Wheel of Fortune," the "Hanged Man," the "Lightning-struck Tower," and "Death." Jungian psychologists are impressed with the universality of such symbols and their divinatory meanings.[10]

Tarot continued to fascinate Europe long after the Renaissance was history. Napoleon carried a pack of Tarot cards during his military campaigns, and always consulted them prior to planning his war strategies. The popularity of fortune-telling with Tarot declined steadily through the Nineteenth Century. The lessened popularity was evidently related to the political decline of France, its champion state.

Tarot is subject to numerous methods of interpretation, but all readings involve the questioner, the reader or interpreter, and the cards. Sometimes the questioner states his question aloud for the interpreter to hear, at other times not. Sometimes the reader has the questioner shuffle the cards, at other times he does it himself. Answers sought from the cards may be either simple "yes" or "no" replies or more inclusive readings. The cards are laid out by the reader in any of several traditional patterns and then interpreted. Obviously, as much depends on the talents of the interpreter as on the order of the cards. The reader may ponder for some time over the cards since there are many possible correspondences.

Each of the seventy-eight cards has some traditional meaning. These meanings are usually flexible enough to allow more than one interpretation (*e.g.* the Death card may imply loss, failure, or mishaps, as well as physical death). In addition, the twenty-two trumps or face cards, unlike our modern playing deck, may be viewed upright from only one direction. The possibility of a card's appearing in the "reversed" position in a reading further extends its possible interpretations (*e.g.* the Death card's "reversed" interpretation may mean recovery from shock or illness). The frequency or proximity of a certain suit's appearance in a reading may also have significance: an abundance of Pentacles usually portends financial matters; Swords, personal strife; Cups, affairs of the heart; Wands, personal advancement.

The Tarot trumps probably gained their special status through a coincidence. There are twenty-two Tarots, and there are twenty-two letters in the Hebrew alphabet. Because all letters in the Hebrew alphabet have numerical meanings, Hebrew is well suited to numerology. Each Tarot card was assigned a Hebrew letter and a corresponding numerical number. This added to the card's magical meaning. One represents unity— God or purpose. Two is the number of light or friendship. Three is the number of totality. Ten is the number of completion.[11]

An Approach to Man's Subconscious?

In recent years Tarot has seen a revival. Creative writers and artists have utilized it as an approach to man's subconscious. T. S. Eliot in *The Waste Land*, Charles Williams in *The Greater Trumps*, William Lindsay Gresham in *Nightmare Alley,* and P. D. Ouspensky in *A New Model of the Universe* have each dealt with Tarot and the subconscious in varying ways.[12] More recently Tarot has been featured in numerous articles on the occult in such national magazines as *Time, Look, Mademoiselle, Playboy, Rolling Stone, Vogue,* and *McCall's*—as well as in a number of recent books on the occult's resurgence.[13]

The entertainment world has also capitalized on Tarot. It has received "leading roles" in movies such as *Games, House of Cards, Isadora, April Fools,* and *Justine.* The record-breaking Broadway rock musical *Hair,* knowing the importance of Tarot cards to the "now generation," has enlarged copies of Tarots as stage settings and passes out Tarot reproductions to the audience during each performance. Charles Ludlau's off-Broadway production *The Grand Tarot* features animated Tarot cards, representing facets of psychotic society, as its entire cast.[14]

Like astrology, the Tarot is used as a way of predicting the future as well as gaining wisdom. It is cloaked in the myths and symbols of ancient ages and seems to offer the security of a link with the past. It meets the need of some people for mystery and hope which technology and the modern church evidently have not met.[15]

This Is Not for the Christian

For a Christian, the Tarot is seen as purely speculation. Furthermore, the Christian realizes that the details of the future are not for man to know. Koch illustrates the danger of prediction by cards in terms of the experience of a young man who went to a fortune-teller. She predicted three events in his life, the third being his death at age twenty-seven. After the occurrence of the first two events, as predicted, the young man lived in total dread of premature death.[16] This illustration makes clear that the details of our futures are not for us to know because of the paralyzing fear that would inevitably accompany such knowledge. God in his mercy has kept the particulars of the future from us. He challenges us, in the meantime, to live a life of faith based on His promise that nothing can tear us away from his love and power and ultimate well-being.

The Bible's strong prohibition of divination raises the question of the origin of whatever genuine predictive ability Tarot might possess. Tarot specialists are vague on this matter. Some contend that Tarot's predictive ability is a product of the personal magnetism and "vibrations" of the reader. Certainly assists from such dubious sources can do nothing to edify a Christian's life.

The Revival of Ouija Board Use

In 1890, Robert Fuld marketed a device known as the Ouija Board. Today it is widely used—especially among young people. The name "Ouija" comes from a combination of the French and German words for "yes." It uses a marker which can move across a board and point towards words that suggest answers. The user places his hand on the plate mounted on tiny wheels with a pencil projecting down from the center and concentrates on the question. Almost imperceptible muscular movements cause the marker to move. Proper utilization requires concentration because these motions result from a low-grade, self-induced trance, close to hypnosis in character.

The Ouija Board has status because the answers recorded seem to come from beyond the power of the operators. The answers have little to do with authentic prediction. They are probably those answers which the user already holds in his subconscious.

Neff states that many people have gotten into serious psychological trouble through the use of the Ouija Board. He warns that they are not "innocent toys." Others believe that "evil spirits" influence the results and purposely lead people into difficult situations.[17]

The Chinese Book of Oracles

The Ouija Board is not the only form of divination popular in America today. Various editions of the Chinese book of Oracles, the *I Ching,* are out-selling Freud and Darwin. Traditional Chinese philosophy sees all of the forces of nature in conflict. Harmony must be achieved through a balance of positive and negative forces. Yang is the name given to positive, masculine, bright forces. Yin forces are negative, female, passive and moist.

This Chinese Taoist philosophy has given way to the occult in a book called the *I Ching* or *Book of Changes.* This book shows all of the possible combinations of yang-yin and the fortunes that will result from each combination. To know the divine will, a person casts coins or sticks, which combine in one of sixty-four hexagrams. These six-line figures, combinations of yang-yin, supposedly show all the possibilities of life.[18]

So far, we have looked at forms of divinations which depend on an intermediary—the palm, Tarot cards, or a Ouija Board. There is another kind of divination that

depends solely upon the charismatic powers of the individual. This type of divination is called intuitive
prophecy.

Divination by Intuitive Prophecy

The priestesses of the Delphic oracle of Greece in-
haled volcanic vapors, went into a trance, and rendered
prophecies. Nostradamus publishd a book of rhymed
prophecies entitled *Centuries* in 1555. He is read by
thousands until today. They claim that he predicted
almost everything that is going to happen until the end
of time. There are some one thousand prophetic qua-
trains in his major work, *Centuries*. They are vague
enough to remain intriguing.

Edgar Cayce is one of the best known of the modern
intuitive prophets. Before his death in 1945, Cayce predicted that by the turn of the century, California would
break apart and slide under the waves of the Pacific
Ocean. His prophecy was remembered after the California earthquake of February 9, 1970. He also predicted many other disasters between 1958–1998. The
East coast will be inundated by melting icecaps, he
predicted. In 1958, geologists discovered melting icecaps.[19] Students of "secular prophecy" are having a
holiday correlating Cayce's time tables with those of
Nostradamus and the contemporary Jeane Dixon.

Located in the strategic city of Washington, D.C.,
Jeane Dixon has become an American legend. She
gained international reputation with her prediction of
the death of President John Kennedy in 1963. She at-
tributes her prophecies to God. Some revelations come
as crystal-clear visions—those are the ones that God
gives to her, she claims.

Not all of Mrs. Dixon's prophecies are dire, but more often than not they turn about the death of a renowned person or a serious calamity. Many of her prophecies are incorrect and embarrassing.[20]

It is true that the Bible prophets also received visions and heard voices. Their prophecies, however, were primarily related to God's redemptive and moral purpose which was to be achieved through his chosen people. False prophets abounded in Israel. They could be recognized because they were not concerned with the moral purpose of Yahweh.[21]

With the prophet Malachi, prophecy ceased for several hundred years. Evidently there was enough recorded writings for the guidance of God's people. In Jesus Christ, God did something new. So new prophets and apostles were inspired to record and interpret the facts and meaning of the life, death, and resurrection of Jesus Christ. New purposes were given to his people—now constituted by the New Testament churches.

The churches later faced heresy. They needed a norm for evaluative purposes. They were led to the decision that only those writings which came out of the apostolic circle and had been regularly read in the churches in the First Century were to constitute the New Testament canon. Jesus Christ and the apostles had brought to a climax the revelations needed. The succeeding generations were not to seek new revelations. Rather, they were to seek to apply to each new generation the meaning and implications of the biblical revelation.[22]

From the evangelical Christian perspective, Jeane Dixon's prophecies are not in the same category as those prophecies in the Bible. The completion of the

New Testament superseded any need for continued direct prophecy. Furthermore, Mrs. Dixon's prophecies are not specifically related to God's redemptive purpose. Her early beginnings were rooted in an interest in the crystal ball, cards, and astrology. Many of her prophecies are related to such things as plays, horse races, and "unlucky" garments. Jeane Dixon is a psychic medium of a superior quality. She is not in the tradition of the biblical prophets.[23]

Obviously, the churches are not opposed to studying trends and planning for the future. Every major denomination has a research office to predict trends in denominational and institutional life. Occult prediction, however, is different from trend projection.

In all fairness, it should be said that neither Jeane Dixon nor Edgar Cayce have claimed to be speaking for God. Perhaps this is different from their claim to have received their gifts of prophecy from God. Would it not be better if they (and their followers) did not claim "supernatural" gifts and be content to see their work in terms of precognition, clairvoyance, and object-reading?

Dixon's "New Messiah" of 1962?

Unger and other conservative authors are very critical of Jeane Dixon's ambiguity in regard to her startling announcement in 1962. She reported that she had a vision concerning a baby who had been born in the Near East. This child was to become a new messiah to set up a new Christianity. By 1969, Mrs. Dixon reversed her interpretation and said that the child was not the new messiah, but the Antichrist. Eventually, after a struggle, Christ will win, she predicted. This, of course, is close to the biblical picture of the last days. Unger claims that the source of her first vision was Satan. Furthermore, extra-biblical prophecies of this nature are not needed. All that the Christian and the world needs to know in matters of faith and practice is in the biblical materials.[24]

Christians should avoid, however, playing the detailed prophetic game with the Bible to the point of setting dates and indicating dogmatic specifics. We must not baptize pagan divination practices and carry them on under biblical labels. The Christian revelation enshrined in the Bible gives enough light for the journey but not enough to satisfy insatiable curiosity. The Bible is a lamp unto our feet—to keep us on the right road and to help us avoid stumbling. It is not a blazing sun to give unnecessary specific details of the far-away mountains. God has promised to care for his children. His revelation concerning the future is not for the purpose of idle speculation. Rather it provides a guide for daily living, a description of definite trends, spiritual power for the journey, and an assurance of ultimate victory. In this sense, the Christian does have an adequate interpretation and prediction concerning the future.

Chapter Seven

CAN I HAVE EXTRASENSORY COMMUNICATION WITH THE LIVING AND THE DEAD?

In the United States we are still living in the aftermath of the Scientific Revolution. We have been conditioned (with our heads) to believe that authentic knowledge can be received only through the five senses. The very word used in the chapter heading—"extrasensory"—is suspect. Most people in technical science have refused to acknowledge the existence of such things as telepathy (communication through no known sensory apparatus), clairvoyance (perception by means other than known sensory apparatus), and precognition (knowing an event will occur before it does). The very mention of the word "ghost" invokes laughter or scorn.

It has been suggested by Richard Woods that this scientific intolerance and almost irrational prejudice is partly responsible for the anti-scientific trends in today's counter-culture. Hypnotism, for example, was rejected by science for years. It therefore survived in the area of the occult and as a stage magician's trick.[1]

In the last few years, however, there has been a subtle but discernible transformation in the scientific attitude toward psychic (lying outside known physical processes) experiences. Several universities have quietly established departments of psychic research. British scientists were somewhat ahead of their American counterparts. The British Society for Psychical Research was established in 1882.[2]

It should be noted that belief in extrasensory perception (ESP) in its various forms (such as telepathy, clairvoyance, and precognition) does not necessarily involve reference to the idea of communication with the dead. The phenomena involved in the question of communication with the dead include apparitions, sensory manifestations of "dead" persons, and "spirit messages" received through mediums. ESP, however, has emerged as a possible clue to the understanding of much that is reported as communication with the dead.[3]

ESP with Living Persons

In the first part of this chapter consideration will be given to claimed extrasensory communication with living people. The possible implications of such communication for the religious concerns of prayer and spiritual healing will be discussed. In the second part of the chapter attention will be focused on alleged extrasensory communication with the dead and related topics such as ghosts, poltergeists, astral projection, and reincarnation.

Some indication has already been given of the meaning of basic terms in the area under discussion. The term "psychic" involves that which lies beyond known physical processes. A shorthand term often used for the general field is the Greek letter *psi* (the first letter in the Greek word, *psyche,* or soul). The prefix *para* is used in the sense of "beyond." Paranormal is an event which is beyond that which present scientific categories define as normal. The study of these events is parapsychology, which is literally "beyond psychology." Psychokinesis is the ability of the mind alone, with no known physical contact, to exercise some control over a physical object. Telepathy is the interaction between the mind (or body) of one person and the mind (or body) of another person by which information is received through no known sensory apparatus. Clairvoyance is the interaction between one person's mind (or body) and a material event by which information concerning the event is perceived by means other than known sensory apparatus.[4]

Psychic research also involves clairaudience (hearing things at a tremendous distance), precognition and retrocognition (knowledge of events from the future or past) and object reading (relating information about a person on the basis of some object they have owned or touched). Included in parapsychology research is levitation (influencing material objects by thought), ghosts, hauntings and automatic writings.[5]

Dr. J. B. Rhine, for many years associated with Duke University, is the most notable early pioneer in parapsychological research. S. G. Soal of London University has also done extensive work in psychical research. Dr. Rhine has had better results with clairvoyant experiments. Dr. Soal's greatest success has been with telepathy.

Things That Go "Bump" in the Day?

Although research still goes on in the area of psychical studies, most fair-minded people will agree that some results have been reached. Even a critical and conservative theologian such as Kurt Koch admits the existence of an area called neutral telepathy. Conservative theologians also emphasize that there is a large body of demonic telepathy. Behaviors studied in laboratories have demonstrated that telepathy and clairvoyance exist. Some extrasensory communication seems to be possible. ESP ability is strongest in children before logical training stunts natural receptivity to ESP. Interest and intelligence often heighten ESP capability. Space and time can be transcended. *Psi* processes seem to work in the unconscious part of our personality. Drugs do not constitute a fast chemical way to become a psychic. There is some, as yet unidentified, force (or forces) that operates in psychic phenomena. It seems to work in healing and in the area of influencing plants.[6]

How Does Telepathy Work?

How does telepathy, for example, work? John Hick believes that it can be said with reasonable certainty that telepathy does not consist of any kind of physical radiation analagous to radio waves. This negation of the physical radiation theory is based on the fact that telepathy is not delayed or weakened in proportion to distance. What happens, according to Hick, is that the sender's thought gives rise to a mental "echo" in the mind of the receiver. This "echo" occurs at the unconscious level. Consequently, the version of the "echo" which rises into the receiver's consciousness may be only fragmentary and may be distorted or symbolized in various ways, as in dreams.[7]

J. S. Wright agrees that the view suggested by Hick is a possible explanation of telepathy. Both of these men utilize the thought of W. Carrington. According to Carrington, our minds are separate only at the conscious level. At the subconscious level our minds are linked even though we are not aware of it. At the unconscious level we are constantly influencing one another. It is at this level that telepathy takes place. Apparently a telepathized thought is directed to one particular receiver by some link of emotion or common interest.[8]

ESP Has Implications for Prayer

It is apparent that ESP has implications for prayer. One model for prayer would suggest that prayer is projection of a mind-force involving extrasensory communication. Frank Laubach maintains that mind-force prayer is normal.[9]

The prospect is frightening, however, unless mind-force prayer is properly utilized. Wrongly used it is close to magic. The Christian model presupposes a personal God. In prayer there is effective communication with him. Prayers of thanksgiving are directed to the Transcendent Father. Prayers of confession result in a communication of forgiveness from him. In prayers of petition, God may assist in granting requests if these requests are good for the one presenting the requests and in keeping with God's overall redemptive purpose. In prayers of intercession, the Transcendent God responds to prayer by ministering to the needs of the prayed-for person. This means that prayer is as basic in Christian work as so-called practical action. The churches need prayer *and* action.[10]

New Testament Safeguards

Christians are fallible men and women. The New Testament tries to safeguard us against selfish or magical prayer by directing us to make our prayers *upward* to God (1 Tim. 2:8) and *in the name of Jesus Christ* (John 15:16). Prayer must be under God's direction and filtered through the mediation of Christ and his plans and purposes. What I will in my own name may be wrong.[11]

Worship is primarily the outgoing of the creature to the Creator. Secondarily, in worship, believers are linked, mind with mind, at the unconscious level. If Christians are intent on one aim, the Holy Spirit finds an effective vehicle for power. If wrong aims are present, the power is retarded. Revival means the removal of wrong aims and attitudes, so that the mind of the church is set wholly on Christ and his purposes.[12]

Psychic healing is a controversial subject. Koch urges that a distinction be made between healing motivated by God and magical healing. People have been healed with the help of both black and white magic. Discernment is urgent. It is obvious that there are healers who exhibit a mixture of characteristics—some from fortune-telling, mesmerism, and magic, and some from Christian sources. In some cases, the healer himself, not God, is exalted as the source of healing power. Koch considered that the techniques used by Oral Roberts in his early healing ministry bordered on the magical approach. Handkerchiefs are used as fetishes by some healers. It is not unusual for the healer to use psychic shock effects. Koch quotes Mark as indicating that wonders incited by demons would appear in the last days (Mark 13:22).[13]

Magic Is Not for the Christian

The Bible abhors magic. In magic healing, a certain relief comes to the body, but the soul is completely bypassed. In the biblical emphasis, man's relationship to God is of far more importance than bodily welfare. According to James 5, healing is always linked with confession of sin and forgiveness. God alone is sovereign. It is he, and not us, who finally decides who is to be healed and who is not.[14]

Following the guidelines suggested by Koch, the work of prominent healers such as Kathryn Kuhlman, A. W. Price, and Olga and Ambrose Worrall should be evaluated. Obviously these healers, and others, possess remarkable psychic gifts. They apparently help people manage organic disease better. It is hard to decide conclusively about their effectiveness in relation to direct organic healing since few diseases are totally organic. Prayer does help the healing process. The ritual laying on of hands also seems to facilitate healing. Enough experimental evidence has been gathered to conclude that some force or energy seems to be mediated through the personalities and hands of some healers. This force may be the factor which swings the balance to recovery in some cases. Remember that the motives and conduct of healers are important. Spiritual healing is not guaranteed. It is obviously a complement to medical healing. To neglect medical healing is to be irresponsible.[15]

The question as to whether or not mind can influence

matter constitutes another controversial subject. Some Christian theologians, including Richard Neff and J. W. Wright, accept the possibility that the mind alone with no known physical contact can exercise some control over a physical object. Neff is impressed with the evidence gathered by Dr. Louisa E. Rhine and presented in her book, *Mind over Matter.*[16]

Kurt Koch and M. F. Unger accept the reality of objects being moved without physical aid (levitation, telekenesis). Their study leads them to state, however, that most cases occur in the vicinity of a medium and in houses where magic has been practiced. Mediums themselves suggest that demonic spirits are involved.[17]

Communication with the Dead

Long before there was extensive interest in extrasensory communication with the living (telepathy), there was interest in communication with the dead. This study, which began in earnest in the late Nineteenth Century, is generally known as Spiritualism. Its opponents who say its manifestations are due to spirit (evil) agency, call it Spiritism. Others say it should not be allowed a term which claims spirituality.

For centuries men have had a deep longing to know whether or not the spirits or personalities of their loved ones have survived in another world. The desperate Saul resorted to a witch to call up Samuel. In 1859, Darwin's work on evolution seemed to put man in the animal column. Evolution, coupled with other scientific developments and a growing materialistic philosophy, raised doubts about life beyond the grave. The time was ripe for Spiritualism.

As with any popular fad, fakes and charlatans took up

mediumship. Houdini, the great magician, exposed many of the mediums. On the other hand, the Society for Psychical Research was begun in London in 1882. It enlisted distinguished names, such as Sir Arthur Conan Doyle, who in turn supported mediums. Arthur Ford, a prominent American minister, became interested and attempted to align Spiritualism with Christianity in the United States.[18]

Parapsychology has been interested, in a general sense, with the theory of personal survival after death for some time. Intense interest, however, has been aroused in recent years by the writings and activities of Bishop James Pike, the flamboyant Episcopal bishop. Through television appearances and books, such as *The Other Side*, Pike has helped to arouse widespread interest in, and give respectability to Spiritualism. A British bishop suggested that Pike visit a medium in order to seek to communicate with his son, Jim. Jim had killed himself in New York City in 1966. Later Pike consulted other mediums. A psychic interview between Bishop Pike and medium Arthur Ford was televised in 1967.[19]

The Growth of Spiritualism

Spiritualism has had a tremendous growth in the last decade. Great Britain has more than 50,000 Spiritualists. In the United States, it is estimated that there are more than 700,000 adherents of Spiritualism. Kurt Koch affirms that there are more than seventy million followers of Spiritualism's teachings in the world. It is a major counter-religion.

In a Spiritualist service, called a seance, contact with the spirit of the departed dead is ordinarily made through a medium or "sensitive." He (or she) is a person who is unusually sensitive to the high-pitched "vibrations" which come from the spirit world. His sensitiveness is seen as a natural gift. Each medium has a contact person known as a "control" in the spirit realm. Communication, therefore, usually involves two on earth and two in the spirit realm.

Not Very Profound Statements

The medium usually goes into a trance. The control in the spirit realm may speak through the medium's vocal cords with his own accent. The conversation between the sitter and the deceased spirit (the "discarnate") is usually trivia such as, "Everything is all right. I am happy. I love you." At the start, details are mentioned to establish credibility. Some details check out as authentic.[20]

Communication from the "other world" may also be in the form of slate writing, rappings to answer questions, table tipping, tumbler moving, Ouija Board movements, or materializations of a body. Photographs have been taken of materialized images. The figures appear to be clothed in something like cheesecloth costumes.

Even if it is granted that there are authentic, though paranormal, experiences involved in a seance, does this prove that the departed spirits are alive and have sent messages? Taken at face value, many seances seem to indicate survival and communication. Apparently, through a medium, one talks with an intelligence who gives an impression of being the loved one who has died. A wealth of private information is oftentimes given.[21]

Several theories have been advanced to explain what

happens in seances. Some say that the seance is a fraud. The material disclosed is based on the medium's investigations. Another theory suggests that the medium uses educated guesses and ambiguous statements until he can gather information from the people in the room.[22]

A Very "Novel" Communication from the Dead!

A more likely theory is based on the power and possibilities of extrasensory perception. The genuine medium is a person of such telepathic sensitiveness that he gathers information from the conscious and subconscious parts of the sitter's mind. Mrs. Eileen Garrett admitted that she used ESP in seances. Kerr calls this the "super-ESP" theory. Two women filled their mind with the characterisics of a fictitious person in an unpublished novel for two weeks. They then went to a reputable medium. The medium proceeded to describe accurately their imaginary friend as a loved one beyond the grave and delivered messages from him.[23]

Closely connected with ESP is the idea of a cosmic consciousness. According to this theory, every event leaves a psychic tracing. The medium can pick up the information from the cosmic mind. There is no loved one sending messages from the "other side." [24]

Of course, the Spiritualists claim actual communication with the departed spirits. Some theologians, such as Neff, state that they cannot completely discount the Spiritualist evidence.

Many conservative scholars, both Protestant and Roman Catholic, contend that the seances represent the intervention of evil spirits. In Spiritualism, this view contends, we encounter demonic powers. Telepathy, of course, could be involved also. Demons seek to deceive and possess humans. The essence of deception is to speak ninety percent truth and ten percent error. Much truth is given in seances. Spiritualism, however, fails to meet the key test of orthodoxy—belief in the divinity of Jesus Christ.[25]

The Biblical Attitude Is Plain

The biblical attitude toward any attempt to communicate with the departed spirits is unquestionably negative. In Leviticus 20:6,27, and Deuteronomy 18:10,11, there are condemnatory references to those who consult a medium who has contact with a control spirit (called a familiar spirit). These passages also condemn wizards (knowing ones) and necromancers (inquirers of the departed).[26]

First Chronicles 10:13 suggests that one of the reasons for Saul's death was his act of seeking a familiar spirit. The story is told in 1 Samuel 28. Saul used forbidden means of inquiry. The prophet Isaiah, as recorded in Isaiah 8:19,20, bitterly condemns spiritualistic practices.[27]

In the New Testament there is absolute silence in the places and circumstances where a Spiritualist could not have been silent. First Thessalonians 4:13–18 states that a Christian is not to sorrow over departed loved ones in Christ, but to wait patiently until the second coming of Christ. First Corinthinas 15:18 implies that we have absolute certainty for Christian survival based on the ressurection of Jesus Christ. There is no need of a seance to prove survival. The Transfiguration was a unique event for a kingdom purpose—not a model for continuing psychic manifestations. The disciples were not told to seek a repetition of the transfiguration.[28]

Nothing About Fellowship with God

From a broad theological perspective it should be noted that Spiritualism says little or nothing about communion or fellowship with God. The real interest of Spiritualism is not in God, but in man. The fact is that the Spiritualist, as such, has no real need for God. Spiritualism also minimizes the atonement and resurrection of Jesus Christ. These facts of the gospel, according to the New Testament, constitute the central biblical basis for restored fellowship with God and hope of personal survival beyond death. From the Christian perspective man's greatest need is to come into a restored relationship with God. Even if personal survival beyond death were proved by the Spiritualists, without a restored relationship to God the person would be in misery. His separation from God, in terms of guilt and insatiable craving, would not be satisfied by moving from this world to another.[29]

Additional theological weaknesses of Spiritualism, from a biblical perspective, can be suggested. In Spiritualism, for example, the foundation of belief is in psychic demonstration, not the Bible. Man is seen as *innately* immortal, and his sin is only against his own progress. Heaven is made into a tawdry "Summerland."

The Theory of the Two Kinds of Ghosts

The reality of ghosts is oftentimes defended by Spiritualists in order to help undergird their teaching about the possibility of conversing with departed love ones. There are two kinds of ghosts—living and dead. G. H. M. Tyrrell has grappled in a serious way with the problem of ghosts in *Apparitions*. A ghost, according to Tyrrell's theory, is the result of a link-up at a deep level of the minds of two or more people. The agent (A) thinks strongly of another person (B). A and B get together and work out a drama that will stimulate the receiving end of B's sense perceptions. In this experience, B will appear, to himself, to see, hear, or feel a hallucination of A. Other people present will be drawn into the drama and will perceive the non-material ghost as though he occupied space. Both departed people and living people can initiate the drama of their appearance. An alternative theory is known as delayed telepathy. In neither theory does the personal spirit actually return.[30]

A popular theory for explaining "hauntings" states that they are caused by the projection of an emotionally charged thought. The thought is projected with such violence in a certain locality that it can be picked up and perceived again and again by certain subjects. Many people, it is affirmed, can sense whether an empty house has been a happy or unhappy house. Carrington suggests that some houses act as an associating object. A new person moving into the house picks up ideas held by the original mind or person associated with the building. Koch contends that a man leaves his spiritual "larva" behind in his house when he dies.[31]

Poltergeists

Poltergeists (noisy spirits) are said to throw stones and move furniture. Some describe such a phenomenon as a projected repression—an extreme form of psychokinesis. Since their activities are usually destructive and disruptive, many see poltergeists as evil spirits at work.[32]

Experiences are reported concerning people who travel during their sleep to distant places. Perhaps this is an example of a person exercising a clairvoyance which transcends space and time.

Most ghosts are harmless thought forms. They are genuine, even though in a sense they are "not really there." Where physical effects are felt as a result of the ghost's activities, explanation seems to be in terms of a semi-materialized mind-force or the activity of an evil-spirit entity. People who commit themselves to Christ will find that the ghosts will retreat as Christ becomes dominant. The Bible itself is silent in regard to any detailed explanation of ghosts.[33]

Communication with the departed spirits is also related to widely held concepts known as the "Aura," "Astral Body" and "Astral Projection." These concepts will be described and evaluated.

They Claim They See Your Aura

Many people with gifts of clairvoyance claim to see an aura (vaporous emanation) around the human body. The size and color of the aura vary because each person has different vibration rates. The aura concept is not new. It has been taught by Eastern mystics for centuries. The nimbus surrounding holy figures often seen in ancient and medieval art is said to represent the aura. The color and composition of the aura surrounding a person tell the clairvoyant observer facts about the health, vitality, morals and disposition of the person observed. Ill health causes the aura to diminish. A dead body has no aura. The aura is said to be caused by mental and physical magnetic forces. Dr. W. J. Kilner of London, England, developed a viewing-glass to better see the aura. Aura goggles are on sale at some occult stores. Drug users report seeing people surrounded by light during a drug trip. Is this related to aura? Edgar Cayce, the famed clairvoyant, used auras to diagnose diseases.[34]

Astral projection and the astral body are more closely related to Spiritualism than is the aura. The classic theory concerning the astral body teaches that a person has two bodily forms—a physical form and a psychical form or an astral body. The astral body is composed of the type of matter that has a higher vibration of matter than does the physical form. Under certain conditions—sleep, trance, coma—the astral body can detach from the physical body and travel. The astral body remains attached to the physical body by a thin lifeline connected to the head or solar plexus. Sylvan Muldoon claims to practice astral travel during sleep almost at will. He travels many places and sees things that he later finds to be authentic when he visits them or sees them in his physical body.[35]

As we have noted, ghosts of living people have been seen by friends many miles away. Perhaps astral projection can be explained in terms of the mind's capacity to extend itself in space and in time. Through this extension it can build up knowledge of what is happening in distant places. This is telepathy plus clairvoyance.

Reincarnation

Reincarnation is an ancient teaching that is related to Spiritualism. It has become an important part of the occult revolution and the counter-culture. Even though the United States is economically victorious, many of its citizens have taken a negative attitude towards its Hebrew-Christian spiritual heritage. From eminent philosophers to "hippies" we are told that we need to turn to the Far East for spiritual help.

A central idea in the Hindu religion and philosophy is reincarnation. Reincarnation presupposes the pre-existence of all souls. These souls are "embodied" throughout history in successive incarnations. The law of Karma or judgment automatically determines the next level of birth on the basis of deeds. The object of the many rebirths is to purify the soul and reach higher and higher levels. The ultimate goal is reunion with the Impersonal God of the universe. Plato, the eminent philosopher of Greece, held a similar theory of reincarnation as have numerous idealistic philosophers through the centuries.[36]

In addition to the interest aroused by Eastern religions and philosophies, discussion of reincarnation was sparked in the United States by the Bridey Murphy case. Morey Bernstein hypnotized Virginia Tighe. Using the age regression technique, she was reportedly taken back into a previous life time. She described episodes in the life of an Irish girl named Bridey Murphy who was born in 1798. Whatever the source, Mrs. Tighe somehow had stored in her mind some unusually accurate information about life in Belfast, Ireland in the Nineteenth Century.[37]

Various explanations of Mrs. Tighe's knowledge have been given. Some critics have attempted to show that her memories of a previous lifetime were really subconsciously preserved memories. These memories were filled with stories told her about Ireland by her aunt and by an Irish lady who lived across the street from her in Chicago during her childhood. Under skilful hypnotic questioning, her imagination had a "field day." The tactic of using age regression to discover information about previous lifetimes is questioned by many hypnotists.[38]

Strange Interviews with Children

More promising evidence for reincarnation comes from a series of spontaneous interviews with children (ages from two to nine or ten) conducted by Dr. Ian Stevenson. Attempts were made to check out details reported by the children in the interviews by a visit to the geographical places mentioned. There were some amazing correspondences. Various theories are given to explain the children's memory of such details. One theory suggests that they drew on racial or genetic memory. Neff favors the possession theory. Possession is the entering of a discarnate personality into a carnate personality and influencing his thought. In other words, the children were possessed by a disembodied spirit who provided the detailed answers which they gave to Stevenson's questions. Dr. Stevenson, the experiment director, favors the reincarnation theory. Both Stevenson and Neff assume that man survives physical death.[39]

Wright suggests that strong emotional experiences could have thrown off elements which linger in space and time. These elements can be sensed by certain sensitive people. There is also the possibility that the children practiced unconscious telepathy or picked up some of the fragments of the world memory.[40]

The Christian turns to the biblical materials to find guidelines to evaluate reincarnation. Jesus obviously

was not teaching reincarnation when he referred to
John the Baptist as the "Elijah which was to come"
(Matt. 11:14; 17:10–12; Mark 9:11–13). In the light of
Luke 1:17, Jesus evidently meant that John the Baptist
would serve God in the spirit and power of Elijah. Fur-
thermore, at the Transfiguration, the disciples had seen
Elijah. He was not John the Baptist.[41]

The Incarnation of Jesus is not to be seen as a reference to reincarnation. Rather Christ is to be seen as the
unique Son of God, the Second Person of the Trinity.
For the Bible, man has only one life to live here on
earth—and it is to be a time of dedicated stewardship
and urgent decision.[42]

A Dangerous Counter-religion

Spiritualism is not only contrary to the Bible, but it
is dangerous as a counter-religion. Spiritualistic forces
are making tremendous inroads as they capitalize on
the interest in Eastern religion and philosophy. A raw
unbridled occultism seems to be sweeping much of the
earth.

Does man survive after death and can we communicate with him? Spiritualism affirms that we can communicate with the departed spirits. Reincarnation
states that man's personality or soul, which now resides
in a material form, has had a preexistence and will be
successively reborn. The biblical answer accepts crea-
tionism. There is no preexistence of the soul. Parents
produce a personal being. This child owes both his
spiritual and physical existence to continued contact
with the progressively creative, transcendent and im-
manent God. Sin disorganizes and separates man from
a saving contact with God. In Christ's atoning death,

forgiveness and removal of sin are provided. In Christ's resurrection, the new life of God comes through to man's spirit. The Holy Spirit dwells in man's spirit upon his conversion to Christ. The power of God continues to hold man's inner being or personality in existence in the presence of Christ at death. Later the personality is given a spiritual body in order that he can find expression, fulfilment and service. The resurrection of Jesus Christ has given the Christian adequate assurance of life after death in Christ's presence so that the Christian does not need to communicate with the departed spirits.[43]

The non-Christian (who has not been made alive by the incoming of the Holy Spirit) is held by God in separation from light and love and fulfilment. The biblical evidence is against universalism (the idea that all men will be saved). Luke 16:23 indicates that the non-Christian's powers are limited and a "great gulf" separates him from possible fulfilment or happiness.[44]

Can We Really Learn Lessons from the Occult?

Granted the presence of heretical teachings and spiritual dangers in the occult, Christianity should not fail to learn lessons from the occult. Man is seeking a positive religion of fulfilment and psychosomatic wholeness. Unless you are somebody first, you have little to offer. The human spirit cannot long remain satisfied with a rationalistic, unemotional, negative approach to life. There must be an experiential appropriation of intellectually known truth, so that it becomes a real dynamic part of life. Although Christianity is based upon history and revelation and an ethical imperative, it also teaches that the Christian life is to be one of wholeness and emotional experience centered in a Christ mysticism.

Evangelical Christianity Has a Superior Alternative

Evangelical Christianity cannot embrace the occult and psychic as such. It can, however, offer the world, from its own resources, a dynamic and superior alternative. It can develop workable methods which will facilitate the appropriation of spiritual resources for practical life. It can affirm the hope that it has for a personal and fulfilling life beyond death. It can tell of the cosmic Christ who embraces all creation. Christianity can and should establish contact with millions of people who have turned to the occult in their search for spiritual meaning.

The recent justice-service emphasis of Christianity must be synthesized with the mystical-experimental resources described in the Bible. The biblical religion can satisfy the fulness of man's religious needs which have been revealed in the occult revolution. Christ has won the victory over the demonic powers. It is the responsibility and privilege of each of us to appropriate that victory in our time!

NOTES

1. Merrill F. Unger, *Demons in the World Today* (Wheaton, Illinois: Tyndale House Publishers, 1971), p. 15.

2. Edward Langton, *Satan, A Portrait* (London: Skeffington and Son, Limited, 1945), p. 117.

3. *Ibid.,* p. 118.

4. *Ibid.*

5. Lambert T. Dolphin, Jr., *Astrology, Occultism and the Drug Culture* (Westchester, Illinois: Good News Publishers, 1970), pp. 19–20.

6. Arthur Lyons, *The Second Coming: Satanism in America* (New York: Dodd, Mead and Company, 1970), p. 1.

7. *Ibid.,* p. 197.

8. Langton, *Satan,* pp. 119–120.

9. Emil Brunner, *The Christian Doctrine of Creation and Redemption,* Vol. II of *Dogmatics,* trans. by Olive Wyon (London: Lutterworth Press, 1952), p. 135.

10. Dale Moody, *Christ and the Church* (Grand Rapids, Michigan: William B. Eerdmans Publishing Company, 1963), p. 138.

11. Lyons, *Second Coming,* pp. 198–199.

12. John Charles Cooper, *Religion in the Age of Aquarius* (Philadelphia: The Westminster Press, 1971), p. 48.

13. Susy Smith, *Today's Witches* (Englewood Cliffs, New Jersey, Prentice-Hall, Incorporated, 1970), pp. 8, 10, 11.

14. *Ibid.,* pp. 13, 14.

15. Richard Woods, *The Occult Revolution* (New York: Herder and Herder, 1971), p. 211.

16. *Ibid.,* p. 16.

17. Dennis Wheatley, *The Devil and All His Works* (New

York: American Heritage Press, 1971), p. 290.

18. Andrew M. Greeley, *Come Blow Your Mind with Me* (Garden City, New York: Doubleday and Company, Incorporated, 1971), pp. 27, 28.

19. Russell T. Hitt, "Demons Today," (Philadelphia: Evangelical Foundation, Incorporated, 1969), p. 12.

20. Woods, *Occult Revolution,* p. 10.

21. *Ibid.,* pp. 10, 11, 24, 184.

22. Greeley, *Come Blow,* p. 33.

23. Brunner, *Creation,* p. 144, Wheatley, *The Devil,* p. 291.

24. Eric C. Rust, *Towards a Theological Understanding of History* (New York: Oxford University Press, 1963), pp. 126, 127.

25. *Ibid.,* p. 127.

26. Helmut Thielicke, *Man in God's World,* trans. and ed. by John W. Doberstein (New York: Harper and Row, 1963), pp. 165–167, 169, 172.

27. Eric C. Rust, *Salvation History, A Biblical Interpretation* (Richmond: John Knox Press, 1964), p. 194.

28. *Ibid.,* pp. 194, 195, 199.

29. *Ibid.,* p. 126.

30. Brunner, *Creation,* p. 143.

31. *Ibid.,* p. 144.

32. Merrill F. Unger, *The Haunting of Bishop Pike* (Wheaton, Illinois: Tyndale House Publishers, 1968), pp. 98, 99, 101.

33. Joseph Bayly, *What About Horoscopes?* (Elgin, Illinois: David C. Cook Publishing Company, 1970), p. 43.

34. George Eldon Ladd, *Jesus and the Kingdom* (New York: Harper and Row, 1964), p. 323.

35. George Eldon Ladd, *A Commentary on the Revelation of John* (Grand Rapids, Michigan: William B. Eerdmans Publishing Company, 1972), p. 98.

36. J. Dwight Pentecost, *Your Adversary the Devil* (Grand Rapids, Michigan: Zondervan Publishing House, 1969), p. 52.

37. Hitt, "Demons Today," p. 12.

38. Karl Heim, *Jesus, the World's Perfecter,* trans. by D. H. van Daalen (Philadelphia: Muhlenberg Press, 1961), p. 189.

39. Arthur F. Smethurst, *Modern Science and Christian Beliefs* (New York: Abingdon Press, 1955), p. 143.

40. G. B. Caird, *Principalities and Powers* (London: Oxford at the Clarendon Press, 1956), p. 70, 71.

41. Ladd, *Revelation,* pp. 98–100.

42. *Ibid.,* pp. 13, 14.

43. *Ibid.,* p. 166.

44. *Ibid.,* pp. 177, 183, 184.

45. Cooper, *Age of Aquarius,* pp. 82, 83.

46. Brunner, *Creation,* p. 145.

47. Woods, *Occult Revolution,* pp. 201–203.

48. Ladd, *Jesus,* p. 323.

49. Donald Grey Barnhouse, *The Invisible War* (Grand Rapids, Michigan: Zondervan Publishing House, 1965), p. 259.

50. Otto Piper, *God In History* (New York: The Macmillan Company, 1939), p. 48.

51. Cooper, *Age of Aquarius,* pp. 83, 84.

FOOTNOTES FOR CHAPTER TWO

1. Smith, *Today's Witches,* p. 45.

2. Woods, *Occult Revolution,* p. 22.

3. Roy B. Zuck, "The Practice of Witchcraft in the Scriptures," *Bibliotheca Sacra,* CXXVIII (October–December, 1971), p. 352.

4. Hitt, "Demons Today," p. 6.

5. *Ibid.,* pp. 6–7.

6. John Stevens Kerr, *The Mystery and Magic of the Occult* (Philadelphia: Fortress Press, 1971), p. 69.

7. Cooper, *Age of Aquarius,* p. 64. Raymond Van Over,

"Witchcraft Today—A Survey," *Witchcraft Today,* ed. Martin Ebon (New York: New American Library, 1971), p. 17.

8. Kerr, *Mystery and Magic,* p. 69.

9. Lyons, *Second Coming,* p. 13.

10. Woods, *Occult Revolution,* p. 98.

11. G. B. Gardner, *The Meaning of Witchcraft* (London: The Aquarian Press, 1959), p. 23.

12. Woods, *Occult Revolution,* p. 30.

13. Lyons, *Second Coming,* p. 14.

14. Kerr, *Mystery and Magic,* p. 71.

15. Woods, *Occult Revolution,* p. 37.

16. Lyons, *Second Coming,* pp. 71, 72.

17. Kerr, *Mystery and Magic,* p. 71.

18. Lyons, *Second Coming,* p. 14.

19. *Ibid.,* p. 32.

20. Kerr, *Mystery and Magic,* p. 78.

21. Woods, *Occult Revolution,* p. 104.

22. Lyons, *Second Coming,* pp. 37, 38.

23. *Ibid.,* p. 43. cf. also R. H. Robbins, *The Encyclopedia of Witchcraft and Demonology* (New York: Crown Publishers, Inc., 1966).

24. *Ibid.,* pp. 58, 59.

25. Woods, *Occult Revolution,* p. 106.

26. Bayly, *What About Horoscopes?,* p. 28.

27. Woods, *Occult Revolution,* p. 107.

Lyons, *Second Coming,* p. 52.

28. Kerr, *Mystery and Magic,* p. 80.

29. Lyons, *Second Coming,* pp. 54, 55.

30. *Ibid.,* pp. 55, 56, 57.

31. Hans Holzer, *The Truth About Witchcraft* (Garden City, New York: Doubleday and Company, Incorporated, 1969), p. 72.

32. Lyons, *Second Coming,* p. 72.

33. Woods, *Occult Revolution,* pp. 111, 112.

34. Lyons, *Second Coming,* pp. 63, 64.

35. Woods, *Occult Revolution,* p. 132.

36. Lyons, *Second Coming,* p. 66.

37. *Ibid.,* p. 69.

38. *Ibid.,* pp. 73, 74.

39. *Ibid.,* p. 79.

40. *Ibid.,* pp. 91–93; cf. also Colin Wilson, *The Occult* (New York: Random House, 1971).

41. Holzer, *The Truth About Witchcraft,* p. 104.

42. Cooper, *Age of Aquarius,* p. 63.

43. Bayly, *What About Horoscopes?,* pp. 37, 38.

44. Lyons, *Second Coming,* p. 113.

45. Woods, *Occult Revolution,* p. 22.

46. Max Gunther, "It Worked for Me," *Witchcraft Today,* ed. Martin Ebon, p. 139.

47. Smith, *Today's Witches,* p. 112.

48. *Ibid.,* pp. 127, 128.

49. Gordon Fleming, " 'Black' Magic Against 'White'," *Witchcraft Today,* ed. Martin Ebon, p. 62.

50. Lyons, *Second Coming,* pp. 115, 116, 117, 118.

51. *Ibid.,* pp. 118, 121.

52. *Ibid.,* pp. 124–126.

53. *Ibid.,* p. 140.

54. Kerr, *Mystery and Magic,* p. 83.

55. Woods, *Occult Revolution,* p. 116.

56. Holzer, *The Truth About Witchcraft,* pp. 129, 131.

57. Kerr, *Mystery and Magic,* pp. 84, 85.

FOOTNOTES FOR CHAPTER THREE

1. Gardner, *Meaning of Witchcraft,* p. 9.

2. Pennethorne Hughes, *Witchcraft* (Baltimore: Penguin Books, 1965), pp. 13, 14.

3. Lyons, *Second Coming,* p. 17.

4. *Ibid.,* p. 143.

5. Woods, *Occult Revolution,* p. 118 f.

6. William Howells, *The Heathens, Primitive Man and His Religions* (Garden City, New York: Doubleday and Company, Incorporated, 1948), p. 127.

7. Raymond Van Over, "Witchcraft Today—A Survey," *Witchcraft Today*, ed. Martin Ebon, p. 20.

8. Lyons, *Second Coming*, p. 143.

9. *Ibid.,* pp. 144, 146.

10. Gardner, *Meaning of Witchcraft*, p. 9.
Hughes, *Witchcraft*, p. 16.

11. Geoffrey Parrinder, *Avatar and Incarnation* (New York: Barnes and Noble, Incorporated, 1970), p. 111.

12. Henry Ansgar Kelly, *Towards the Death of Satan* (London: Geoffrey Chapman, 1968), pp. 111, 112.

13. Kerr, *Mystery and Magic*, p. 82.

14. Kurt E. Koch, *Between Christ and Satan* (Grand Rapids, Michigan: Kregel Publications, 1970), pp. 61, 62.
Merrill F. Unger, *Demons in the World Today* (Wheaton, Illinois: Tyndale House Publishers, 1971), pp. 79, 80.

15. Koch, *Between Christ and Satan*, p. 78.

16. Smith, *Today's Witches*, p. 6.

17. *Ibid.,* p. 14.

18. Koch, *Between Christ and Satan*, pp. 82, 93.

19. Holzer, *The Truth About Witchcraft*, p. 214.

20. Unger, *Demons in the World Today*, pp. 92, 93.

21. Smith, *Today's Witches*, pp. 17, 92.

22. *Ibid.,* p. 93.

23. Raymond Van Over, "Witchcraft Today—A Survey," *Witchcraft Today*, ed. Martin Ebon, p. 16.

24. Smith, *Today's Witches*, p. 95.

25. *Ibid.,* pp. 96, 98.

26. Koch, *Between Christ and Satan*, p. 83.

27. Smith, *Today's Witches*, p. 99.

28. Koch, *Between Christ and Satan*, pp. 74–78.

29. Roy B. Zuck, "The Practice of Witchcraft in the Scriptures," *Bibliotheca Sacra*, p. 355.

30. *Ibid.*

Woods, *Occult Revolution,* p. 100 f.

31. Lyons, *Second Coming,* pp. 356–357.

32. *Ibid.,* p. 358.

33. Roy B. Zuck, "The Practice of Witchcraft in the Scriptures," *Bibliotheca Sacra,* pp. 358, 359.

34. Unger, *Demons in the World Today,* pp. 80, 81.

35. H. Richard Neff, *Psychic Phenomena and Religion: ESP, Prayer, Healing, Survival* (Philadelphia: The Westminster Press, 1971), p. 162.

36. *Ibid.*

37. *Ibid.,* pp. 162, 163, 165.

38. *Ibid.,* pp. 166, 167.

39. Emile Cailliet, *Why We Oppose the Occult* (Philadelphia: University of Pennsylvania Press, 1931), p. 178.

40. *Ibid.,* pp. 178–183.

41. Kerr, *Mystery and Magic,* p. 86.

42. Ron Matthies, *The Unopened Door: Christianity Facing the Occult* (Minneapolis, Minnesota: Augsburg Publishing House, 1971), p. 88.

43. Woods, *Occult Revolution,* p. 187.

44. Jean Stafford, "Love Among the Rattlesnakes," *McCalls,* March, 1970, p. 146.

45. Kerr, *Mystery and Magic,* p. 86.

46. *Ibid.*

47. Lyons, *Second Coming,* p. 156.

48. Woods, *Occult Revolution,* pp. 180–182.

49. Eugene A. Nida and William A. Smalley, *Introducing Animism* (New York: Friendship Press, 1959), p. 57.

50. Woods, *Occult Revolution,* p. 125.

51. Kerr, *Mystery and Magic,* p. 87.

FOOTNOTES FOR CHAPTER FOUR

1. Woods, *Occult Revolution,* pp. 124, 125.

2. J. Stafford Wright, *Mind, Man and the Spirits* (Grand Rapids, Michigan: Zondervan Publishing House, 1971), p. 129.

cf. J. L. Nevius, *Demon Possession and Allied Themes* (New York City: Fleming H. Revell Company, 1893), and Leslie D. Weatherhead, *Psychology, Religion and Healing* (New York City: Abington Press, 1951), pp. 94–97.

3. M. Thomas Starkes, "Hog Fat on Anxiety," *Home Missions*, XLIII (January, 1972), p. 11.

4. "Lying Spirits and Teachings of Demons," *Home Missions*, Interview with Kent Philpott, p. 44.

5. Koch, *Between Christ and Satan*, p. 133 f.

6. *Ibid.*, pp. 133, 134.

7. James Kallas, *Jesus and the Power of Satan* (Philadelphia: The Westminster Press, 1968), pp. 202, 203, 212.

Weatherhead, *Psychology, Religion, and Healing*, pp. 52–60.

8. C. H. Dodd, *The Authority of the Bible* (London: Nisbet and Company, Limited, 1928), pp. 236–37.

9. T. K. Oesterreich, *Possession Demoniacal and Other: Among Primitive Races, in Antiquity, the Middle Ages, and Modern Times*, trans. D. Ibberson (New York: Richard R. Smith, Incorporated, 1930), p. 11. cf. also S. V. McCasland, *By the Finger of God* (New York: Macmillan Co., 1951).

10. Ladd, *Jesus and the Kingdom*, pp. 145–147. cf. also Weatherhead, *Psychology, Religion and Healing*, pp. 89–94.

11. Wright, *Mind, Man and the Spirits*, pp. 128, 129.

12. James Kallas, *The Satanward View, A Study in Pauline Theology* (Philadelphia: The Westminster Press, 1966), p. 133.

13. Kurt E. Koch, *Christian Counseling and Occultism* (Grand Rapids, Michigan: Kregel Publications, 1965), p. 19.

"Lying Spirits and Teachings of Demons," *Home Missions*, p. 45.

14. Koch, *Christian Counseling and Occultism*, p. 184.

15. *Ibid.*

16. Oesterreich, *Possession Demoniacal and Other,* pp. 38, 47, 89, 94, 105, 136, 182, 183.

17. *Ibid.,* pp. 63, 96.

18. Kurt E. Koch, *Occult Bondage and Deliverance* (Grand Rapids, Michigan: Kregel Publications, 1970), p. 186.

19. *Ibid.,* pp. 195, 196. cf. Weatherhead, *Psychology, Religion and Healing,* p. 97 f. for the opinion that possession is indicated.

20. *Ibid.,* p. 205.

21. Koch, *Christian Counseling and Occultism,* p. 17.

22. *Ibid.*
Koch, *Occult Bondage and Deliverance,* p. 133.
Weatherhead, *Psychology, Religion and Healing,* p. 99 f.

23. Koch, *Christian Counseling and Occultism,* p. 208.

24. Oesterreich, *Possession Demoniacal and Other,* pp. 3, 77, 114, 208.

25. *Ibid.,* pp. 269, 94, 379, 217.

26. *Ibid.,* pp. 54, 80.

27. Koch, *Occult Bondage and Deliverance,* p. 160.
Koch, *Christian Counseling and Occultism,* p. 217.

28. *Ibid.*
Koch, *Occult Bondage and Deliverance,* p. 166.

29. Koch, *Christian Counseling and Occultism,* pp. 217, 218.

30. Koch, *Occult Bondage and Deliverance,* p. 148.

31. Wright, *Mind, Man and the Spirits,* p. 132.

32. Koch, *Occult Bondage and Deliverance,* p. 137.

33. *Ibid.,* p. 148.

34. *Ibid.,* p. 138.

35. *Ibid.,* pp. 138, 139.
"Lying Spirits and Teachings of Demons," *Home Missions,* p. 44.

36. Koch, *Occult Bondage and Deliverance,* pp. 139, 148.

37. *Ibid.,* p. 139.

38. Koch, *Christian Counseling and Occultism*, p. 219.

39. *Ibid.*

40. *Ibid.*, pp. 219, 220.

41. *Ibid.*, p. 220.

42. *Ibid.*, p. 223.

43. *Ibid.*, p. 224.

44. *Ibid.*

45. *Ibid.*, 225.

46. *Ibid.*, pp. 225, 226.

Koch, *Occult Bondage and Deliverance*, pp. 149, 150.

47. Wright, *Mind, Man and the Spirits*, p. 131.

48. Koch, *Christian Counseling and Occultism*, p. 227.

49. *Ibid.*, pp. 230, 231.

50. *Ibid.*, pp. 231, 232.

51. *Ibid.*, p. 232.

52. *Ibid.*, pp. 233, 234.

53. *Ibid.*, 235.

54. *Ibid.*, p. 236.

55. *Ibid.*, p. 240.

56. *Ibid.*, p. 241.

Koch, *Occult Bondage and Deliverance*, pp. 187, 188, 189.

57. Koch, *Christian Counseling and Occultism*, p. 189.

58. "Lying Spirits and Teachings of Demons," *Home Missions*, p. 45.

59. Koch, *Christian Counseling and Occultism*, pp. 242, 243.

60. *Ibid.*, pp. 244, 248, 249.

61. *Ibid.*, pp. 237, 238, 251.

62. Koch, *Occult Bondage and Deliverance*, pp. 87, 88, 254, 256.

63. Koch, *Christian Counseling and Occultism*, pp. 258, 259, 260, 261.

64. *Ibid.*, p. 265.

65. *Ibid.*, pp. 267, 270.

Koch, *Occult Bondage and Deliverance*, pp. 91, 94.

66. *Ibid.,* p. 102.

Koch, *Christian Counseling and Occultism,* pp. 270, 271.

67. *Ibid.,* pp. 271, 272, 273.

68. *Ibid.,* pp. 274, 275.

69. *Ibid.,* pp. 277, 278.

"Lying Spirits and Teachings of Demons," *Home Missions,* p. 45.

70. Koch, *Christian Counseling and Occultism,* pp. 281–285.

71. Koch, *Occult Bondage and Deliverance,* pp. 67–71.

72. Koch, *Christian Counseling and Occultism,* pp. 290, 291.

FOOTNOTES FOR CHAPTER FIVE

1. Dolphin, *Astrology, Occultism and the Drug Culture,* pp. 10–17.

2. Sybil Leek, *Diary of a Witch* (New York: New American Library, Incorporated, 1969), p. 168 f.

3. Louis MacNeice, *Astrology* (Garden City, New York: Doubleday and Company, Incorporated, 1964), pp. 12, 13.

4. "Astrology: Fad and Phenomenon," *Time,* March 21, 1969, p. 47.

5. Selma Robinson, "Maurice Woodruff: Astrology's Brightest Star," *McCall's,* March, 1970, p. 76.

6. Kerr, *Mystery and Magic,* p. 14.

7. *Ibid.,* p. 15.

8. Nicholas Pileggi, "Occult," *McCall's,* March, 1970, p. 140.

9. Kerr, *Mystery and Magic,* p. 13.

10. "Astrology: Fad and Phenomenon," *Time,* March 21, 1969, p. 48.

11. MacNeice, *Astrology,* pp. 10, 30, 189.

12. Kerr, *Mystery and Magic,* p. 40.

13. Woods, *Occult Revolution,* pp. 69, 88, 93.

14. "Astrology: Fad and Phenomenon," *Time,* March 21, 1969, p. 48.

15. Kerr, *Mystery and Magic,* pp. 23 f., 39.

Jacob Needleman, *The New Religions* (Garden City, New York: Doubleday and Company, Incorporated, 1970), p. 197 f.

16. "Astrology: Fad and Phenomenon," *Time,* March 21, 1969, p. 48.

17. Dolphin, *Astrology, Occultism and the Drug Culture,* pp. 7, 8.

18. "Astrology: Fad and Phenomenon," *Time,* March 21, 1969, p. 48.

Woods, *Occult Revolution,* p. 94 f.

19. Kerr, *Mystery and Magic,* p. 62.

20. Woods, *Occult Revolution,* pp. 63, 65.

21. "Astrology: Fad and Phenomenon," *Time,* March 21, 1969, p. 53.

22. *Ibid.*

Kerr, *Mystery and Magic,* p. 17.

23. *Ibid.*

Woods, *Occult Revolution,* p. 65 f.

"Astrology: Fad and Phenomenon," *Time,* March 21, 1969, p. 53.

24. *Ibid.*

25. Woods, *Occult Revolution,* pp. 69, 70.

26. *Ibid.,* pp. 67, 62.

27. Kerr, *Mystery and Magic,* p. 18.

28. *Ibid.,* p. 19 f.

29. *Ibid.,* p. 21.

30. Koch, *Between Christ and Satan,* p. 12.

31. *Ibid.,* p. 13.

32. Kerr, *Mystery and Magic,* p. 31.

33. Dolphin, *Astrology, Occultism and the Drug Culture,* p. 13.

34. Kerr, *Mystery and Magic*, p. 32 f.

35. "Astrology: Fad and Phenomenon," *Time*, March 21, 1969, p. 56.

36. Matthies, *The Unopened Door*, pp. 22, 28.

37. Kerr, *Mystery and Magic*, p. 34.

38. "Astrology: Fad and Phenomenon," *Time*, March 21, 1969, p. 56.

39. Woods, *Occult Revolution*, pp. 88–90.

40. Kerr, *Mystery and Magic*, p. 35 f.

41. "Astrology: Fad and Phenomenon," *Time*, March 21, 1969, p. 56.

42. Kerr, *Mystery and Magic*, p. 20 f.

43. *Ibid.*, p. 23.

44. Koch, *Between Christ and Satan*, p. 15.

45. Koch, *Christian Counseling and Occultism*, p. 80 f.

46. Kerr, *Mystery and Magic*, p. 23.

47. *Ibid.*, p. 38.

48. Koch, *Christian Counseling and Occultism*, p. 78.

49. Koch, *Between Christ and Satan*, p. 12.

50. Starkes, "Hog Fat on Anxiety," *Home Missions*, p. 7.

51. Koch, *Between Christ and Satan*, p. 18.

52. Kerr, *Mystery and Magic*, p. 41.

53. Koch, *Between Christ and Satan*, p. 18.
Dolphin, *Astrology, Occultism and the Drug Culture*, pp. 11, 16.

54. Kerr, *Mystery and Magic*, p. 42.

55. MacNeice, *Astrology*, p. 142.

56. Koch, *Between Christ and Satan*, p. 18.

FOOTNOTES FOR CHAPTER SIX

1. Kerr, *Mystery and Magic*, p. 47.

2. *Ibid.*, p. 47 f.

3. *Ibid.*, p. 50.

4. Matthies, *The Unopened Door,* p. 68.

5. *Ibid.*

6. *Ibid.,* p. 69.

7. Koch, *Between Christ and Satan,* p. 26.

8. Matthies, *The Unopened Door,* p. 71 f.

9. S. R. Kaplan, *Tarot Cards for Fun and Fortune Telling* (New York City: U.S. Games Systems, Incorporated, 1970), p. 9.

10. Eden Gray, *The Tarot Revealed* (New York: Bell Publishing Company, 1960), p. 2.

11. Kerr, *Mystery and Magic,* p. 53 f.

12. Gray, *Tarot Revealed,* p. 2.

13. Cf. John Godwin, *Occult America* (Garden City, New York: Doubleday and Company, Incorporated, 1972).

14. Dorothy Powills, "Tarots and Your Future," *Hobbies,* August, 1970, p. 122.

15. Matthies, *The Unopened Door,* p. 56.

16. Koch, *Occult Bondage and Deliverance,* p. 20.

17. Neff, *Psychic Phenomena and Religion,* p. 131.

18. Matthies, *The Unopened Door,* p. 16.

19. *Ibid.,* p. 79 f.

20. Woods, *Occult Revolution,* p. 165 f.

21. Wright, *Mind, Man and the Spirits,* p. 169.

22. *Ibid.,* p. 173.

23. Unger, *Demons in the World Today,* p. 63 f.

24. *Ibid.,* pp. 69–71.

FOOTNOTES FOR CHAPTER SEVEN

1. Woods, *Occult Revolution,* p. 173.

2. *Ibid.,* p. 173 f.

3. John Hick, *Philosophy of Religion* (Englewood Cliffs, New Jersey: Prentice-Hall, Incorporated, 1965), p. 54.

4. Neff, *Psychic Phenomena and Religion,* pp. 17, 28.

5. Woods, *Occult Revolution,* p. 175.

6. Kerr, *Mystery and Magic,* p. 92 f.

Neff, *Psychic Phenomena and Religion,* pp. 154–157.

Cf. also J. B. Rhine, *The Reach of the Mind* (New York: William Sloane, Inc., 1947).

7. Hick, *Philosophy of Religion,* p. 55.

8. Cf. W. Carrington, *Telepathy* (London: Methuen and Company, Limited, 1945), Chaps. 6–8.

9. Wright, *Mind, Man and the Spirits,* p. 163.

10. Neff, *Psychic Phenomena and Religion,* p. 86.

11. Wright, *Mind, Man and the Spirits,* p. 163.

12. *Ibid.,* p. 165.

13. Koch, *Between Christ and Satan,* pp. 143–152.

Koch, *Occult Bondage and Deliverance,* p. 52.

14. Koch, *Between Christ and Satan,* pp. 152–154.

15. Neff, *Psychic Phenomena and Religion,* pp. 89–113.

16. *Ibid.,* p. 156.

Wright, *Mind, Man and the Spirits,* p. 80 f.

Cf. Louisa E. Rhine, *Mind Over Matter* (New York: The Macmillan Co., 1970).

17. Koch, *Between Christ and Satan,* p. 107 f.

Unger, *Haunting of Bishop Pike,* pp. 68–71.

18. Kerr, *Mystery and Magic,* pp. 94–96.

19. *Ibid.,* p. 103 f. cf. James A. Pike, *The Other Side* (Garden City, New York: Doubleday and Company, Incorporated, 1968).

20. *Ibid.,* p. 98 f.

21. Hick, *Philosophy of Religion,* p. 56.

22. Neff, *Psychic Phenomena and Religion,* p. 121 f.

23. Hick, *Philosophy of Religion,* p. 56.

24. Neff, *Psychic Phenomena and Religion,* p. 124.

25. Wright, *Mind, Man and the Spirits,* p. 109.

26. *Ibid.,* p. 105.

27. *Ibid.,* p. 105 f.

28. *Ibid.,* p. 106 f.

29. *Ibid.,* p. 112.

30. *Ibid.,* p. 115. cf. G. N. M. Tyrell, *Apparitions* (New Hyde Park, New York: University Books, 1961).

31. *Ibid.,* p. 116 f.

Koch, *Occult Bondage and Deliverance,* p. 115.

32. Wright, *Mind, Man and the Spirits,* p. 118.

33. *Ibid.,* p. 120 f.

34. *Ibid.,* p. 98 f.

Kerr, *Mystery and Magic,* p. 112 f.

35. Wright, *Mind, Man and the Spirits,* p. 92 f.

36. Woods, *Occult Revolution,* p. 177.

37. Neff, *Psychic Phenomena and Religion,* p. 144.

38. *Ibid.*

39. *Ibid.,* pp. 145–150.

40. Wright, *Mind, Man and the Spirits,* p. 138.

41. *Ibid.*

42. *Ibid.,* p. 139.

43. *Ibid.,* pp. 147–175.

44. *Ibid.,* p. 176.